SAINT PAISSY (VELICHKOVSKY), THE HOLY ELDER OF MOLDAVIA

LIFE

DOCTRINE OF MENTAL OR INNER PRAYER

Sergius Jumati and Irina Veris

Gozalov Books
The Hague

This book has the blessing of
His Eminence Simon, Archbishop of Brussels and Belgium
and temporarily of The Hague and the Netherlands

ISBN: 978-90-79889-13-6
Translation from the Russian original "Преподобный Паисий (Величковский), святой старец Молдавский

Editor: Mother Superior Lydia Portaïtissida, Trazegnies, Belgium, portaitissa@skynet.be
Translation: Theodore (Wilfred) Rosdorff
Abridged from: "Doctrine of mental or inner prayer" and the explanations: Guram Kochi and Irina Veris
Corrections: Guram Kochi
Illustrations and the photo of the icon on the cover: the aquarelles by Natalia Komarovskaya-Jumati
Design: Guram Kochi and Marijcke Tooneman

Tel.: 00 31 (0) 70 352 15 65
E-mail: gozalovbooks@planet.nl
Website: www.hetsmallepad.nl

Table of Contents

List of Illustrations

Author's introduction

"Lord, Jesus Christ, Son of God, have mercy on me! If anyone repeats this prayer longingly and incessantly, like breathing through the nostrils, soon the Holy Trinity - Father, Son and Holy Spirit - will settle in him, will create an abode in him. The prayer will devour the heart and the heart - the prayer. The person will start to say this prayer day and night and will liberate himself from the enemy's nets. Indeed, you should pronounce the prayer to Jesus like this: Lord, Jesus Christ, Son of God, have mercy on me. Whether you stand, sit, eat, travel, or do something else – continuously pronounce this prayer. Fervently urge yourself to pray it, because it strikes invisible enemies, like a warrior's strong spear. Impress it in your thoughts; and do not be shy to secretively repeat it in lavatory too. And when you have exhausted your tongue and mouth, then pray with your mind only."
Venerable Païssy (Velichkovsky)

The legacy of the holy fathers undeniably testifies: the foundation of true spiritual life is unceasing inner prayer. Metropolitan Hierotheos (Vlachos), one of the modern, Greek zealots of piety in the spirit of the patristic tradition, writes: "The purpose of the Jesus prayer is to win Christ, the kingdom of Jesus, in the heart. We open the kingdom of God within us by kindling the spark of grace, which is now hidden under the ashes of sin. And then our plea in the prayer comes true: Thy kingdom come. But now... the heart is obscured by the darkness of sin and demons are at work in it. The Evil One established his dominance over the heart (but not over its centre, because only the action of the Holy Spirit, Who is uncreated, unites with the soul, and supervises all)... Praying we strive first that the mind would assimilate the sweetest name of Jesus, then Christ in all His glory and splendour will descend into the heart and will banish the evil spirit that darkens the soul with various passions even after the soul has received God's grace which protects it (the soul). So, through the coming of Christ the soul becomes enlightened, receiving grace upon grace. The more the Lord draws near, the more the Evil One moves away, with a shout and a cry of defeat he suffered. The echoes of these screams are temptations, induced by him." Such, one might say, is the overall picture of the spiritual, unseen warfare, which is part of the life of every Christian, and especially of every monk.

In the instructions of venerable Ephraim the Syrian, one of the great spiritual masters of the IVth century, we read: "The primary Work of a monk is [preserving] silence, that is, life without amusements, away from all worldly concerns, so that having outgrown human enjoyments, he will cleave to God. The second Work is well balanced fasting, that is, to eat once a day some ordinary food, and not to satiety. The third Work is well balanced vigil, that is, to spend a half of the night in psalmody, sighs and tears. The fourth is psalmody, that is, bodily prayer, consisting of [singing] psalms and kneeling. The fifth is spiritual prayer, performed in the mind, therewith warding off all extraneous thought. The sixth is reading the lives of the Holy Fathers and their instructions, not to lend an ear to alien teachings, or anything else to conquer the passions with the help of the words of the fathers. The seventh is to seek the advice of experienced fathers about any word and undertaking, so that the monk because of his inexperience and self-assurance, his thinking one thing and doing another, will not perish when the flesh rages as a result of demonic slander or wine... So all must be proportional in order not to undermine zeal by lack of moderation."

There happened not so long ago in the Pskovsko-Pecherski Monastery of the Holy Dormition of the Theotokos the following. A monk called Michael went through the hard ordeals of the war years and when he came to the monastery, he became an exemplary monk: as a man of prayer and a hard worker he distinguished himself by humility and obedience. By profession he was a carpenter, and his work of obedience was making reliquaries, lecterns and crosses. One day, after finishing an icon case in the refectory of the monastery, he suddenly fell unconscious. His heart stopped beating and he stopped breathing. The monastery doctor, who came running when being called, confirmed he was dead. But then Father John Krestiankin, the father-confessor of the monastery, looked at Michael and said: "No, he's alive," and began to pray. Michael awoke, burst out crying and asked to be taken to his cell. The next day, monk Michael began to entreat the superior of the monastery to tonsure him into the great schema, and he received it with the schema-name Melchizedek. On adopting the schema he changed his life: he started to work less and pay more attention to prayer. Once they asked the schemamonk, "Father Melchizedek, what did you see that moment when we thought you were dead?" And he said: "I saw myself standing in a beautiful meadow, and in front of me a huge ditch filled with dirt. And in that ditch was all my carpentry: all the lecterns, crosses, reliquaries I've ever made. I looked at it horrified. And I suddenly felt that someone was standing behind me, I turned around and saw the Mother of God. She said: "That's all that will remain after you. Now you see where it will end up. You're a monk; We've been expecting repentance and prayer from you and look now: here is what you brought Us." The Lord brought Father Melchizedek back to life. As before he faithfully fulfilled his work of obedience, but now he has been confessing that the most important things for a monk are repentance and prayerful communion with God. His prayer has been since then quite remarkable. Many people came to this schemamonk when seeking help.

His deep inner prayer also helped him to bear the heavy cross of disease.

The great elder [here and further on in the text the word "elder" is used in the meaning of "spiritual mentor, leader, guide"], venerable Païssy Velichkovsky apparently had the special gift from God to understand that the Lord expects from a monk in the first place repentance and prayer. In his sermon entitled "Lilies of the field or beautiful flowers," he writes: *"What should be done so that the mind is always occupied with God? If you do not acquire these three virtues: love of God and people, abstinence and Jesus prayer, then your mind cannot be fully occupied with God; for love tames anger, lust is weakened by abstinence, and prayer diverts the mind from thoughts and banishes all hatred and haughtiness. Indeed, be constantly occupied by God, for God will teach you everything and He will reveal by the Holy Spirit the highest, the heavenly, and the lowest, the earthly. Amen."*

This ascetic of the XVIIIth century was ranked among the assembly of the saints 200 years later, in 1988. It was absolutely not by chance that he was glorified and canonized by the Russian Orthodox Church in the year of the 1000th anniversary of Christianity in Russia, after which came a time of restoration of churches. Venerable Païssy re-entered the life of the modern Christian, he became a spiritual mentor, not only of monks but also of laymen.

Eras of relative spiritual impoverishment alternate with periods of spiritual flourishing. But if you look closely, in every century can be seen ascetics, whose example always makes the spiritual life of the era more brightly visible. These people sanctified the path for their contemporaries, revealed to them the will of God; through them and around them the church was built and that what is eternal, divine in the church was created. In different periods a particularly vivid spiritual life could be concentrated in certain areas. "We see that countries, cities, nations, regions and monasteries alternate, but the general life of grace is flowing undisturbed. When halted in one place, it flares up in another, sometimes spreading more widely, sometimes concentrating in a small circle of people, it never dries out, but it renews itself and renews those in each generation who respond to the call of truth," writes priest Sergius Mansurov in his book "Essays on the history of the church".

The narrow monastic path of venerable Païssy Velichkovsky was a spiritual mission of the same strength in the XVIIIth century as the asceticism of venerable Sergius of Radonezh in the XIVth century. These elect of God had to work hard because these were historical periods in which it was difficult to accomplish monastic works. Inspired by the heritage of the holy Fathers of antiquity, they - by the grace of God - have become bearers of spiritual experience, trained many disciples and transformed in this way the general spiritual climate of their era.

Archpriest Sergius Chetverikov wrote about venerable Païssy Velichkovsky the following: "If all the work of the holy elder had only been setting an example of personal holiness, the establishment of a monastic coenobitic community on the ancient patristic foundations and the correction of patristic books, then also in that case this work would not have been unimportant for the church, monasticism and society. But the holy Elder Païssy did more than that: he established a school of spiritual life, he inspired a wide spiritual movement in monasticism, he kindled the hearts of many with love for the spiritual life, kindled the aspiration to accomplish inner monastic feats, to spiritual labours. Under the influence of Elder Païssy Velichkovsky many remarkable hermits were trained in orthodox monasticism, and they fully assimilated the precepts of the holy elder. Through constant prayer, unremitting observation of oneself, self-examination, internal struggle with one's thoughts, confession of thoughts, obedience and humility, diligent study of the treaties of the holy Fathers, and the observance of the evangelical commandments, they reached a high degree of spiritual life. They acquired a great influence not only on their brethren, monks, but also on the laity, sometimes even highly educated in the secular, as well as in the theological sense. Having started in the second half of XVIIIth century, this spiritual movement continued to grow throughout the whole XIXth century until the very revolution."

The first edition of "The Life of the Moldavian holy Elder Schema-archimandrite Païssy Velichkovsky" was published in 1847. With this publication the publishing work in Optina was started. Indeed, the Optina Monastery – of the Holy Presentation in the Temple near the town of Kozelsk, in the Kaluga eparchy, that became famous in the XIXth century - acquired its spiritual significance due to the pupils of the Saint Païssy.

The hagiography presented to your attention, is compiled from different editions, but at the base of it is the text of archpriest Sergius Chetverikov, "The Moldavian holy Elder Païssy Velichkovsky, his life, teachings and influence on orthodox monastic life" (1938). It should be noted that the questions elucidated in this book are relevant also in our time. The author hopes that this work will bring spiritual benefit both to monks and laymen.

With the love of God, Sergius Zhumati
Saint-Petersburg, January 2010

CHAPTER 1. THE HEIR OF THE POLTAVA ARCHPRIESTS

The home of the future "Moldavian holy Elder" is the city of Poltava in the Ukraine. In his early youth he left these parts, but until the end of his days he remembered them, he retained his ability to speak Ukrainian and in his letters and writings he loved to add the words "native of Poltava" after his signature.

St. Païssy descended from a pious family of hereditary priests. In the Velichkovsky family living a life in the service of orthodoxy began with his great-grandfather Luke, who was ordained an archpriest[1] of Poltava. His grandfather, father and elder brother were also appointed rectors of the cathedral of the Dormition of the Most Holy Theotokos in Poltava.

His maternal grandmother was the Mother Superior of the Convent of the Protective Veil. Irene, the pious mother of the future hermit, later took the veil in the same monastery and received the name Juliana.

The righteous man was born on December 21, 1722 on the feast day of the holy hierarch Peter, metropolitan of Kiev and Moscow and wonderworker of All Russia (†1326). At baptism the infant was named Peter. When he turned 4, his father, archpriest John, died. Peter remained in the care of his mother and his elder brother John.

From an early age Peter's favourite pastime was reading. He attended the church school at the cathedral where he learned to read the ABC, the Book of Hours and the Psalter. In due time, Peter read all the religious books which could be found at home and in the cathedral library: the Old and New Testament, the lives of the saints, the teachings of Saint John Chrysostom, Saint Ephraim the Syrian, and others. From reading these holy books, particularly the hagiographies of the venerable fathers, the desire was born in his soul to leave the world and become a monk. He grew unusually silent and was completely immersed in his inner life. At the same time he was neither gloomy nor despondent; his face was joyful and friendly.

When Peter turned 13, his elder brother John died. John had been rector of Poltava's cathedral for five years. His mother wanted to keep the place of priest for her son, Peter. She was given letters of support by Peter's godfather colonel Kochubey and other honourable citizens, and with these she, her son and his uncle went to Kiev, to Archbishop Raphael Zaborovsky. Poltava was within the jurisdiction of the archbishop at the time. His eminence blessed Peter, and said: "May you be the successor". After that he gave a confirmation deed of inheritance of the rector's chair and gave them a farewell blessing, ordering to immediately send the boy to study at the Kiev theological academy. The "Kiev fraternal colleges", where Peter was told to go, was at that time a rather complex educational institution. It was a combination of elementary, middle and high schools placed within the walls of the Theophany Monastery, under the general name of the Kiev-Mogyljnskaya Academy of the Theophany. Here they taught Latin, Polish, Greek, Slavic languages, rhetoric, theology, philosophy and music.

Peter studied at the academy for three years, and through his prayerful communion with God in the depths of his soul, an inner transformation took place: a desire grew strong to fully devote himself to serve the Lord after completely renouncing the world. His first mentor was hieroschemamonk Pachomius of the Theophany Monastery. He had spent many years on pilgrimage and at one time lived in the desert. Father Pachomius gave Peter books from his library; besides that, he had long- edifying conversations with him, which strengthened Peter's decision to join a monastery. He began to realize that in the matter of the salvation of the soul, besides faith, it is

necessary to diligently keep the commandments of Christ. So Peter set for himself the following three rules: 1) not to condemn one's neighbour, even if you see him sinning with your own eyes, 2) not to harbour hatred to anyone and 3) to forgive offences with one's whole hart. As Elder Païssy wrote : "My commitment to keeping these commandments, given to God, I could indeed not keep because of my negligence, but with God's help I followed these commandments in the spirit of the true teachings of the Scripture, and I will follow them on this comfortable and unlaborious path; after all, there is no other path to salvation."
During the third year of his education his zeal for schoolwork began to weaken, and the desire of monasticism absorbed his whole being. The sudden disappearance of two of his friends broke off the last thread that bound Peter to the Academy. He supposed that they had left for the Kitaevo Hermitage of the Kiev Monastery of the Caves. He chose a convenient time and set out to visit this holy community. His friends were indeed there. They warmly welcomed Peter and spent that evening together reading a book of venerable Ephraim the Syrian. The next day after the Liturgy Peter was invited by the head of the hermitage, hieroschemamonk Theodosius, to the common fraternal meal. The reverential atmosphere made a deep impression on Peter: he felt as if he were sitting among God's angels, as if he were not on earth but in heaven. After the meal, the friends again had a long conversation with him and urged him to renounce the world, to end his studies at the academy and to take the vow of obedience in the monastery. He was ready to do it, but he was afraid that his mother, as he well knew, would never consent to his entry into the monastery. On the third day he said goodbye to his friends, and returned to the academy and continued his studies, but no longer with any zeal.

During the first two years at the Academy Peter went to his native Poltava for the summer. At home he read books and attended the services in the cathedral. But in the summer of 1738 he stayed in Kiev and lived in Podol near the church of the Holy Hierarch Nicholas the Good, in the house of an old widow who loved him and cared for him as her own son. Taking advantage of his free time, Peter went around the sacred places, churches and monasteries of Kiev. He regularly went to the church of holy Sophia, the Wisdom of God to venerate the relics of the holy Metropolitan Macarius of Kiev, and to the monastery of the Archistrategos of God Archangel Michael to venerate the relics of the Holy Great Martyr Barbara. And what can we say about the impact on his young soul of the holy and great Kiev Monastery of the Caves! He loved this sacred and God-chosen place with his whole soul. Here shone venerable Anthony and Theodosius and all the holy fathers of the Caves like the ancient God-bearing fathers. They were "earthly angels and heavenly human beings", who during their lives as well as after their death glorified God by their miracles and their incorruptible relics! He usually attended the Divine Liturgy there on Sundays and public holidays. Sometimes he would also go in the evenings and spend the night with the pilgrims in the Near Caves. Seeing the splendour and ecclesiastical discipline, and the multitude of honourable monks, Peter's soul rejoiced. It seemed to him that in the church had gathered the venerable Fathers of the Caves themselves, and he praised God for the given opportunity to often visit this holy place. At the end of the divine service, he would enter the caves to honour and to kiss the holy relics and the myrrh-shedding heads of the saints. The silence and stillness in the caves, which cannot be found above ground, kindled in his soul the unrealizable desire to stay in these sacred caves, not to leave the relics of the venerable fathers...

Peter made an agreement with the guard of the monastery, and on Saturday evenings and before the major feasts he could meet his friends from the Kitaevo Hermitage. They would gather at the gates on the territory of the Monastery of the Epiphany and would discuss the important question of how they could carry out their intention and find such a / monastery where God would be favourably disposed towards them to be tonsured into monasticism and to live by monastic vows? During these conversations there grew in their souls the firm understanding that there could not be any renunciation of the world in monasteries that have an abundance of food and drink and all sorts of bodily comfort. They decided to find such a monastery, where it is possible to take monastic vows that prescribe to follow the poverty of Christ, to live in abstinence, and to tame the flesh for the sake of the salvation of the soul. Otherwise, they reasoned, it is better to be in the world and married according to Christian law than, having renounced the world be obliged to satisfy the flesh and spend a life in abundance thereby profaning the monastic ideal and risking the eternal damnation of the soul. Thus conversing, they sat for nights, until the beginning of the church rule, and after the service they parted and left for their homes.
Peter grew exceptionally fond of the Kitaevo Hermitage. The modest wooden church dedicated to the great hermit Venerable Sergius of Radonezh, the deep silence and stillness of this place: everything there was arranged for prayer and pacified the soul. One day, when he again crossed the threshold of the cloister, he saw the head of the hermitage, standing near the church. Peter bowed before him to the ground and asked for his blessing to stay in the cloister and to make his monastic vows. Father Theodosius ordered him to follow him. He took him to his cell and sat down on the bench at the table and said to Peter: "Brother, sit down here," pointing with his hand at a chair, standing nearby. The chair was higher than

the bench on which sat the head of the hermitage. Sensitive as Peter was, he was troubled by this proposal. He blushed deeply, bowed politely, and remained standing. The superior told him to sit down on the chair a second time. Peter bowed to him and remained standing. The same proposal was repeated a third time. Peter did not budge. Then Father Theodosius said, "Oh, brother, you implore me to accept you in my hermitage as a monk. But in your heart I do not see a trace of monastic disposition, I do not see in you the humility of Christ, I do not see in you either obedience, or cutting off of your will and reason, but I see all of the opposite. I see in you the inner state and sophistication of this world, I see in you the pride of the devil, I see in you disobedience, and compliance to your own will and reasoning. Three times I told you to sit next to me and you did not obey. You would need to renounce all your own will and reasoning, with humility and fear of God listen to me, if I would ask you just one time. And now here, in my cell, I asked you thrice, but you followed your own will and reasoning and violated my commandment, pretending hypocritically to be submissive and bowing with the pride of the enemy. Without obedience and cutting off of your will, which are the signs of a true monk, how dare you ask me to accept you into monasticism? Those who are not obedient and follow their own will and reasoning are not worthy of the monastic way."

But after this stern rebuff, the head spoke to Peter with love and gentleness, like a father to his son: "For the love of God, I specially led you into this temptation, because I wish your soul to be saved. Now your soul will remember your whole lifetime that the true basis of monasticism, the root and foundation of the path to God, is obedience and cutting off of your will and reasoning.

Blessing of the Father Superior

All who wish to be worthy of the monastic way leave behind them the world and everything which is of the world. They also have to cut off all their will and reasoning and in everything render obedience to their mentor on the path to God, even until their last breath, as to God Himself. But do not be dismayed about this temptation. Be forgiven by God and by me, a sinner."

Father Theodosius began to question Peter about where he was born and whether there were not any obstacles for him to take the monastic vows. The youth briefly explained everything. "My beloved son" said Father Theodosius, "even if you beseeched me and begged me to take you into this hermitage as a monk, after your story I do not dare to do so. In what situation would we find ourselves, if your mother should find out where you are? She could take you from here by order of the authorities. But do not lament over yourself. Keep a constant desire to join a monastery, entrust everything to the care of God and with His help diligently seek to find such a place, where there will be no obstacle to the monastic life for you. I assure you, God Almighty wishes the salvation of all and He will guide you to such a place and will fulfil your desire." Peter prostrated himself before Father Theodosius and asked forgiveness and after receiving a blessing, he left the hermitage.

In September classes began at the academy, but Peter was no longer interested in studies. He attended the lessons less and less regularly. His mind was constantly troubled by the thought of finding a suitable place for the monastic life.

In late January, one of the students, who saw that Peter did not attend classes, went to the rector of the academy, Sylvester Kulyabko[2], and told him that Velichkovsky was not studying, and that thus his mother was spending her money in vain. When the rector heard this he sent two students to Peter. When they brought him, he asked him for what reason he left his studies and he received the following answer: "The first reason is that I have a firm intention to become a monk and as I am aware of the truth that the hour of death is unknown, I want to take monastic vows as soon as possible. The second reason is that in this academic teaching I do not see any benefit to my soul, as is printed in the spiritual Alphabet of holy hierarch Demetrius of Rostov: "Now it is not by the Holy Spirit, but by Aristotle, Cicero, Plato and other pagan wisdom-lovers that the intellect is instructed. They are fully blinded by lies and lured away from the righteous path towards reason. They teach just empty thoughts. In their souls are shadows and darkness, and all their wisdom is only of the tongue." So I don't feel that this study is beneficial for my soul, and I fear to fall for a perverted mind, so I stopped learning it. Finally, the third reason is the following: I examined the fruits of that teaching in spiritual people, in monks, and I saw that they live as a kind of secular dignitaries, in great honour and glory, and in all kinds of bodily comfort. They adorn themselves with precious vestments; they ride in good horse-drawn sledges. Without condemning them, I say: I do not want that to happen to me. I have spent quite a long time at these studies. And the longer I spend at them, the more I will suffer when I will have become a monk, because the more I will fall into mental and physical passions. It is for these reasons I stopped with these studies."

The rector was a wise mentor, so in the conversation he patiently began to explain to Peter that academic education is also of great benefit, and if he does not understand this, it isn't surprising, since he barely touched the studies. The greatest Church Fathers, like the holy hierarchs Basil the Great, Gregory the Theologian and John Chrysostom diligently studied heathen poets and philosophers. This ancient wisdom will not prevent him from becoming a true monk, as it did not prevent the great holy Fathers becoming the leading lights of Orthodoxy and true servants of Christ. However when he realized that Peter did not accept his exhortations and remained unbending, he became angry and threatened him with corporal punishment for disobedience. But he saw the feebleness of Peter and feared that the stubborn student might fall ill, so he decided not to touch him and commanded him only to study at least until the summer. "Then," he said, "You will be free to follow your intention, without any obstruction from the governing body of the academy." The youth accepted this offer and patiently continued the fourth year of studies at the academy.

While in Kiev he regularly met his confessor, hieroschemamonk Pachomius. From him he could borrow books. To give food to his soul he copied whole pages out of them and then often re-read these in order to confirm his aspiration to enter a monastery.

In the summer, Peter went to his mother in Poltava. Soon after his friend Demetrius came to visit him. He was following a course at one of the colleges in Kiev. In spirit he held the same views as Peter. He also wanted to enter a monastery. Meetings and conversations with him kindled such a burning desire in Peter's soul to become monk, that he decided to tell his mother everything: that he can't be the rector of the cathedral, like his ancestors, that he will not finish his education at the academy and, the most important, that he will leave her and go on a pilgrimage to seek a monastery where he will take the monastic vows.

One can only be amazed at how strong Peter's desire must have been, that he was not afraid to do this. Because his dear mother had hoped that Peter would become the archpriest of Poltava, continuing the family tradition , that he would be her support and comfort in her old age, that she would have the occasion to hold her grandchildren. She had twelve children, and only Peter remained, to continue the Velichkovsky bloodline.

Upon learning of Peter's intention to leave for the monastery, his poor mother began to weep and mourn. Peter tried to console her, explaining that she should rejoice and praise God, who had given him such an intention. But his words and arguments did not help. From day to day, more and more, she became sick from grief. Peter went to his confessor and told him everything as it was.

To comfort his mother the confessor advised him to talk with her more cautiously. When he returned home, Peter said to her that first he would continue to study, not to remain a boor, who cannot preach the word of God, that he wanted to be a strong preacher like his great-grandfather, grandfather, father, and brother. Upon completing his education, may be God would favour him to become father superior and preacher. Listening to his words, his mother gradually calmed down in the hope that her expectations would be fulfilled.

The time to prepare for the journey to Kiev came. Peter, knowing that there wouldn't be any studying for him, packed his things just for appearances' sake so that his mother would not suspect anything. When all was ready for departure, his friend Demetrius, with whom he intended to set off to a monastery, suddenly fell ill, so Peter left for Kiev alone. His Mother accompanied him to Reshetylivka, a hamlet, located 30 km from Poltava. Her mother's heart felt that she was seeing her

son for the last time. She started crying, begging him not to leave her, to study diligently at the academy and every summer to travel to Poltava. Peter, aware that he was parting from his mother forever, also wept. He fell at her feet, begged for his mother's forgiveness and blessing, while in tears kissing her hand. She blessed him, and they parted. Ambivalent feelings possessed him: he mourned, thinking of his mother, and he rejoiced about his liberation from the bonds of the world.
Upon arrival, Peter wrote to his mother that with God's help and through her prayers, he had successfully reached Kiev. He decided to go for advice to hieroschemamonk Pachomius, who was in the city of Chernigov then, together with his Eminence Metropolitan Anthony. Thus the first step for the realization of his plans was taken.
At that time, the son of a priest was planning to go home by the same road. The young men decided to travel together and hired a boatman.
By God's providence Peter was protected on the way to Chernigov. Here is what he wrote about this voyage: *"Having called on the aid of God, we crossed the Dnieper, and went up the river Desna. Who can recount the distress, which I suffered on this journey? The month of October was very cold. My companions had enough warm clothes not to notice the cold. But I left all my clothes in Kiev and had taken only the minimum. I was shaking with cold, especially when there was rain and snow. Even at night, when we pulled the boat ashore and lit a big fire, I could not get warm. While one side was warmed, the other was frozen. And so it went on all night, and I could not sleep. My companions however were sleeping quietly. Because we rowed against the stream, we always had to pull the oars. My companions were in good health and had strength, so they could cope with it.*

On the way to Chernigov

Whereas I, feeble from birth, never having worked physically in my life, worked beyond my strength, which made my whole body, especially hands and feet, terribly hurt. All over my body, under my clothes, countless lice multiplied and were biting me. At night, when my companions were asleep, I shook my things above the fire, thereby gaining a short rest from their attacks. But the worst thing for me was the fear of drowning. The boat in which we travelled was very small, it barely held the three of us. The sides were only three or four fingers above the water. And when the river was choppy, the cold water simply swept over the sides of the boat, and I had to constantly bail out the water. That was the only way we could save ourselves. Sometimes, in the middle of the river, the boat would hit a bank, and then we would jump out, and holding the boat, would bail out the water. The river washed away the sand from under our feet, almost sweeping us to the depths. I nearly went mad from fear that the river would swallow me. Only by sending up prayers to God and trusting in His grace, did we get over these sandbanks."

When on the tenth day of the trip they came close to the town of Ostyor, they saw a man coming down to the river. Later it turned out that this man, Daniel Shatilo, saw they were in a dangerous situation. Having come down to the bank near the boat, he began to reprimand the boatman, "Didn't you fear God when you took these young people on your little cockleshell on such a long journey on such a large river? You're an old man, you have lived a life and you are not concerned with death. But to take these young people with you... wouldn't it be a sin on your soul if they drowned? In exchange for this labour of yours you are not worthy of any payment, but you are worthy of severe punishment, as a murderer." With such words he led them to his home, where the young travellers could rest for a few days. Peter's companion paid half the price to the boatman, saying: "halfway, half the price." But Peter, so as not to upset the old man gave him the fee for the entire way to Chernigov.

Daniel, who sheltered them, found a good oaken boat that was sailing to Chernigov. He sent Peter and his companion off on this boat, and paid for them. They thanked Daniel and they continued their way. The owners of the boat fed them and looked after them. A few days later, they arrived safely in Chernigov. The young men went ashore, and their ways parted.

In the archbishop's house, Peter found priest-schemamonk Pachomius. Peter lived with him in his cell, and all the time Peter kept asking him for counsel and advice: where to go on a pilgrimage? After a few days Father Pachomius said to Peter: "If you want with all your zeal to go on a religious pilgrimage for the sake of following the monastic way, then the best for you is to go to the monastery, which is not far away from the city of Liubech. It is the birthplace of our venerable Father Anthony of the Caves. In the monastery you will find priest-schemamonk Joachim. And it is to him you should appeal. This monastery is situated on the banks of the Dnieper. And if your desire will be to continue on your pilgrimage, a more convenient place to start your journey cannot be found. Wait a few more days, until someone else is going to that area and I'll arrange that you will profit by this opportunity." Peter managed to find a man who was travelling to that territory, unfortunately, though not all the way to Liubech, but only up to his own village which was not far away from the town. Bidding farewell, Father Pachomius said to Peter: "Do not sorrow, the Lord is strong, and He will lead you safely to the monastery." Receiving a blessing for the road, Peter rode off. They arrived when it was already dark, and the youth stayed overnight at the home of his guide. Peter was afraid to walk alone; the road ran through woods where predators lived. However in the morning, despite Peter's repeated requests, the man refused to guide him to the monastery. Putting all his trust in God, he set out on the way alone.

Walking out into the open field, Peter saw the town of Liubech ahead, and the dome of the monastery at a distance of about a couple of kilometres from the town. Approaching the monastery, he became extremely worried as the road from the river Dnieper was blocked by obstacles, and the only remaining passage to the monastery was guarded. Peter did not have any documents, so he approached the guards, and began to pray to the Lord with all his heart. Obviously it was according to God's providence that a monk just walked out of the monastery and came up to the outpost.

"Who are you?!" The guard sternly asked Peter. To this, all of a sudden the monk replied: "Why you ask, "Who are you?" don't you see that it is a novice? He did his work of obedience and now returns to the monastery." The guard let Peter pass without further questions. Having thanked God, Peter and the monk, who's name was Father Arkady, walked into the monastery.

Looking through the window of his cell, Father Arkady asked Peter, "Look, do the hegoumens in Kiev dress like ours?" Peter looked through the window and saw an old man, grey-haired, in a threadbare black cassock, in appearance a simple monk. The young man was struck by such modesty and he said to Father Arkady: "Since my very birth I have not seen the head of a monastery dressed so shabbily." Father Arkady brought him to the hegoumen, whose name was Nicephorus, and, having kneeled, according to custom, they both received his blessing. "Where are you from, brother? What is your name and why have you come to our monastery?" asked Hegoumen Nicephorus. "My name is Peter. I come from Kiev, yearning to become a novice in a monastery," replied the young man. "I thank the most merciful God who has sent you to us in obedience," said the hegoumen. "Two days ago, our only novice, also named Peter, left the monastery, and there was no one to whom I could give the cellarer's[3] obedience. To you, who have the same name, I appoint this obedience." The hegoumen led Peter to the pantry. He showed all that was available, assigned him his responsibilities and lodged him in a cell not far from his own.

Peter fulfilled this obedience with joy, but his health suffered. Several times a day he had to take off the heavy wooden lid from tubs and put it back in place, move heavy bags, keep the storehouse in order and deliver products to the monastery kitchen. He did not dare to complain to the hegoumen about the labour that was beyond his strength and he continued to humbly perform this obedience. He wanted as soon as possible to wear black monastic clothes. And it happened that an old monk passed away. The hegoumen told the novice: "You might want to take his clothes to wear." It was a cassock made of thick grey cloth, but for Peter it was an ineffable joy. At night, in his spare time, he visited priest-schemamonk Joachim, to whom Father Pachomius had sent him. Together they read the cell prayer rule and talked.

After some time priest-schemamonk Joachim was assigned to live in the hermitage of ascetic Onuphrius, located five kilometres from the monastery. The hegoumen gave Father Joachim's cell to Peter and, caring for his spiritual development he gave Peter the book by Venerable John of the Ladder (Climacos), saying: "Take this book, brother, and diligently, carefully read it. Learn more about holy obedience and how to fulfil good works, because this book is very good for the soul." Peter liked the book so much that at night he copied it for himself, using a burning splinter as source of light.

Soon the first monastic temptation befell novice Peter. The brethren of the monastery saw his soft, forgiving nature and began to misuse it. They visited Peter asking from him food for them: flour, millet, barley. Peter could not say "no", and though tormented by his conscience, he gave away products without the blessing of the hegoumen.

Sometimes during the meal the hegoumen would ask Peter to read the lives of the saints. At times he read with such feeling that many of the brethren were moved, wept, and some even would get up from the table and stand around Peter listening to him, in tears. This touched the young novice profoundly. But the greatest joy for his soul was the fatherly love of the hegoumen who governed the brethren with gentleness, humility and patience. If one of them had sinned and asked forgiveness, the hegoumen would forgive him, explain him his transgression, and assign him a penance[4] fit to the strength of the offender. With such a wise and meek mentor the brethren lived in harmony, constantly thanking God.

Three months passed. And then, by order of Anthony, Metropolitan of Moldavia, who then ruled the Chernigov eparchy, Hegoumen Nicephorus was transferred to another monastery and a certain Father Herman (Zagorovsky), was assigned as the Father Superior of the Liubech monastery. Unlike the former hegoumen, Father Superior Herman ruled imperiously, without any love or mercy. Some of the brethren, discerning the character of the new hegoumen, left the monastery. Peter decided to do his best to comply with the requirements of the new Father Superior.

During the Great Fast, the hegoumen commanded Peter to give the cook cabbage to cook a meal. The novice did not understand however what cabbage exactly he was talking about, but being shy he was afraid to ask again. He suggested to the cook that he pick the cabbage himself for the hegoumen's table.

"Did I command you to supply this sort of cabbage for my table?" said the incensed hegoumen and, not waiting for an answer, struck Peter on the cheek, so that he could hardly remain on his feet. Then he pushed him out the door and shouted: "Off you go, lazybones!" Trembling with fear, Peter asked himself that if for such a trifling offense the hegoumen treated him so cruelly, what would happen in the event of a serious blunder.

During this time, the cell-attendant of the hegoumen also did something wrong. The enraged Father Superior threatened to punish both of them severely. The monks who heard this warned Peter, and when Peter told this to the cell-attendant, the latter proposed to run away from the Liubech monastery. In the sixth week of Lent, sending up prayers to God, they left the monastery under cover of night and walked along the bank of the Dnieper. In the villages they found good people who did not refuse to shelter the two pilgrims, to give them food, and to let them dry their clothes and warm themselves. Finally, they reached the river Pripyat, which was covered by a thin layer of ice. Would they be able to get over this melting, thin ice to the other shore, or would they fall through into the cold deep? At that time, some people approached the shore. All together, helping each other, they cautiously crossed to the other side after which they sat down to take a breath. And then before their eyes the ice began to break with a loud crack across the whole river and to float downstream: the spring ice drift had started. The pilgrims fell to their knees and with inner trembling thanked the Lord. Having prayed they walked into the town of Chernobyl without difficulty, as there were neither fences nor guards, and soon they found shelter.

It was Lazarus Saturday. The next morning, walking down the street, Peter heard someone calling him by name. Looking back, he saw a fellow townsman from Poltava who warmly greeted them and invited Peter, together with his friend to his house. The fellow townsman told Peter that he came to this city on behalf of Colonel Basil Kochubey to purchase wood. He also told Peter that his mother was crying and sobbing inconsolably, and many residents of Poltava also grieved for him.

Many years later, his sister-in-law – the wife of his deceased brother, archpriest John – told him about what happened to his mother. After Peter's departure his mother's heart could not find peace. She cried all the time and waited for news from him, which would confirm that he was indeed continuing his studies at the academy and that he was all right. But there were no letters. Then she quickly packed up her things and went to Kiev. Unable to find Peter at the academy, she went round all the monasteries and hermitages of Kiev and the district. He wasn't to be found anywhere, and no one could tell her where he had gone. She returned home, where for several days she cried incessantly, day and night, refusing the food and drink that was offered to her by her relatives, who assembled around her. All her hopes and expectations that were placed on her only son were lost, her nerves could not stand such a blow, and she started talking to herself, answering questions inappropriately: mental derangement set in. She didn't have the strength to get up from bed. The relatives nursing her one day suddenly witnessed an unusual phenomenon: some frightening vision distorted her face, her hands moved nervously. She begged to be given the Akathist to the Mother of God. She took the book and after reading a few pages out loud, she fell silent and lay still. The relatives tried to take the book from her hands, but they couldn't because she was holding it tightly. They thought that she had probably had a terrible vision, and had protected herself by reading the Akathist. Then they managed to carefully take the book out of her hands and began to read it aloud, and they continued reading the Akathist incessantly many times.
A day and a night passed. Suddenly she opened her eyes and gazed upwards without moving them as if at something which only she could see. After an hour had passed her said loudly: "If this is God's will, I will no longer grieve for my son." The relatives were looking astounded at her begging her to

tell them what had happened. But she still hadn't come to herself and she only asked them to call her confessor. When he arrived, she confessed, and came back to her senses, but she was completely exhausted. Her relatives fed her with a spoon, like a small child.

A bit strengthened, she sat on the bed and talked about her ordeal: "I was so weakened by my emotion and hunger that I thought I was going to die soon. But then I was surrounded by hordes of terrifying, dark demons, who wanted to grab me and drag me to hell. That's when I asked you to give me the Akathist to the Mother of God. When I started reading, the demons started to tremble with fear and retreated. They did not dare to come near me. That's why I did not give you the book, I was afraid they would attack me. A day later, thanks to the intercession of the Mother of God, I suddenly saw the heavens open and an angel of God like a bright flash of lightning come down from heaven and stand beside me. " Oh, wretched woman," the angel said to me, " what are you doing to yourself? Instead of loving Christ your Lord and Creator with your whole soul and with all your heart more than all creation, you love your son more than Him. For the sake of your love for your son you choose to die and to expose yourself to eternal damnation. Even if your son had gone the way of robbers, or whatever other wicked way, even then it would not be fitting for you to grieve immeasurably, because on the Day of Judgment everyone will be responsible for himself. Your son has chosen the monastic life by the will of God, so are you allowed to grieve so desperately and to waste your soul? Let it be clear to you that by God's grace your son will surely be a monk. You also ought to follow his example and cease to mourn, renounce the world and become a nun. Such is God's will. If you're going to oppose it, and grieve and mourn for your son, then I will give you to the devils. They are waiting for you, to treat your soul and body with their usual lawlessness as an example to other parents, so that they will not love their children more than God!" So then I said: if it be the will of God, I will no longer grieve for my son. And the angel of the Lord, rejoicing, ascended to heaven."

With the help of God Peter's mother completely recovered and, remembering the vow she had made to the Lord, began to prepare to enter the Pokrovsky Convent, located five kilometres from Poltava.

But at that moment in Chernobyl the fellow townsman of Peter was telling him that his dear mother is crying inconsolably and began to persuade him to return. The unexpected meeting made Peter uneasy. He was haunted by the idea that they could arrest him and take him home. Because of his worries he ate nothing for lunch. The same day, he decided to leave the city. Wasting no time, Peter walked to the nearest church school to find out if there was somebody going to right bank Ukraine. There he met a monk who was going to go to the south-western territories. With great difficulty Peter persuaded the monk to take him with him and he left with the monk alone, so he did not wait for his companion.

The pilgrimage brought Peter a lot of suffering. From walking so long, his left leg ached and was swollen up to his knee, so he moved with great difficulty and frequently had to stop to rest. The monk wanted to leave him in the first village they came to on their way, but Peter's pleading softened his heart, and they continued on their way together, but they had to spend two or three days in every village where they stopped for lodging. It took a little time, and the leg healed. After a while the pilgrims came to a small hermitage called Rzhychiv. This hermitage belonged to the Saint Cyril Monastery in Kiev. They asked the father superior of the monastery the blessing to stay some time to recuperate.

But instead of rest a new challenge befell Peter here: he fell gravely ill. Even eating a little made him vomit. After a month of this, he was so weak that he could not get out of bed. He constantly prayed to God, pleading not to let him die in this hermitage, since he had not yet managed to realize his intention.

By God's providence three wandering monks came to the hermitage. They were on their way to Moldavia. When Peter heard this, he begged them to take him along with them. The monks seeing his extreme weakness and sickliness, at first refused, but later they consented to his plea. On hearing this good news Peter gained strength, and when they left the monastery and walked up the hill, he almost felt completely healthy.

But trials continued to pursue him, as some kind of new Job: on that same day there was a terrible thunderstorm. His travelling companions quickly ran ahead to find some accommodation, but he was still weak and did not keep up with them. He was caught in a field by rain that turned into large hailstones, the size of walnuts. It was late at night when he reached the village where his companions had taken shelter, and he only found them the next day. When the monks saw Peter in health and unharmed, they were sincerely glad: their conscience had tormented them for having abandoned the sick and feeble Peter in a storm in the open field.

They began to think of which way they should go to Moldavia, and they asked around. The local deacon told them: "I advise you, holy fathers, not to go to those regions. There are soldiers travelling along all roads now to catch robbers, and if you fall into their hands, they may treat you cruelly out of hatred for our orthodox faith. In our village recently a deacon, the one before me was killed," and he told them how it had happened. The monks were horrified to hear such a story, and decided to head down the Dnieper, hoping to settle in one of the monasteries along the river.

The pilgrims approached the Moshensky Mountains. In one village, they met a hieromonk[5], who told them about an anchorite called Hesychius, who lived on an island in the river near the mountains. The two monks continued their way but Peter decided to visit the anchorite. The hieromonk took him there. Peter saw that the anchorite was working diligently for the salvation of his soul; he was copying the books of the holy fathers. He concluded that if he became a disciple of Hesychius, then the ascetic would set him on the path of salvation. Peter asked him to accept him as a novice. Hesychius replied: "I am a sinful man and full of passions, and not worthy to be your spiritual mentor. I cannot even set my own destitute soul on the path to God. How could I dare to take you as an apprentice? That is beyond my powers. Please do not try to persuade me anymore." Peter thought that it was out of humility that he did not want to take him as a disciple, so with even greater force he began to ask for it. But Hesychius rejected his pleas.

Peter returned to the village, but the inner desire to settle with that pious anchorite made him once again go to Hesychius. And again, feeling a deep sense of embarrassment, not daring to look him in the face, Peter fell on his knees and tearfully asked Hesychius to take him into obedience, saying: "Holy father, accept me for the Lord's sake. I will obey you in everything, like God himself. If I am disobedient in anything, throw me out as if I were a stinking dog." He wept so bitterly, that Hesychius, seeing the utter dismay of Peter, said to him: "I beseech you, for God's sake, my brother, do not be grieved about this. I do not accept you for the sake of your salvation because of the weakness of my soul. God who knows the hearts of all is a witness to that. Set all your hopes on the All-powerful providence of God. He will not leave you, as you are sincerely seeking salvation. With His grace He will comfort

your tears, and He will guide you on the straight and narrow path."
Peter went back to the village and found a place to stay with a good Christian. He did not know what to do next. The hieromonk, who had led him to the anchorite, was not in the village. Peter decided to return to Hesychius to ask for advice. When he came to the recluse, he begged him to let him stay until the Lord would set him on the right path. To the measure of his powers, Peter fulfilled his obedience. A few days later the hieromonk arrived. The anchorite asked him to take Peter to some monastery.

Having visited several monasteries, he came to the monastery of the Saint Archbishop Nicholas, known as Medvedovsky, on an island in the river Tyasmina. The father superior, hieromonk Nicephorus, accepted him in the monastery, placed him in a cell with another novice, and blessed him to fulfil the daily monastic obedience common to all the brethren. It was summer, the month of July. In the monastery they were storing up hay, after that they harvested the crop; they transported the sheaves to the threshing-floor. Peter had great difficulty doing these jobs. When reaping, he would cut his fingers; shipping the sheaves, he would make a cart topple over. The brethren at first rebuked him, but seeing that it was no use, they gave Peter the duty of bringing clay and water by cart to the threshing-floor. Apart from that, he received a blessing from the hegoumen to sing in the choir and to work in the refectory. All this Peter did very willingly, rejoicing in the fact that he could serve the brethren.

It should be noted that in a monastery idleness is totally unacceptable. This is indicated by the holy fathers, warning that idle pastime in the cloister leads to the development of passions and corrupts the monk. This particularly applies to those who are not yet spiritually trained, those who have barely started on the path of monastic life. In each monastery

the correct combination of work and prayer is of no small importance. The fathers called work and prayer the two wings, with which those who are labouring for their salvation raise high in the abode of eternal life.
In the month of August, when the Dormition fast started, the hegoumen called Peter to him and said: "I have decided to tonsure you and the second novice, who shares your cell, as rassophore. So go to the confessor, confess and prepare yourself for the Eucharist. Also visit hieromonk Nicodemus and ask him to be godfather at your tonsure." Peter feeling both fear and joy went to the confessor. He confessed his sins, received absolution and the blessing to prepare to partake of the holy Eucharist of Christ. He then went to hieromonk Nicodemus. "Are you asking me this yourself, or with the blessing of the hegoumen?" asked Father Nicodemus. Learning that the hegoumen had given Peter the blessing, he promised to be his godfather. He told him only to wash his hair for the day of tonsure. That was very much to the point indeed, as Peter had not had the opportunity either to wash or even to comb his hair since the day he had left the Liubech monastery about five months ago.
On the day of the feast of the Transfiguration of the Lord, after reading the Hours, the tonsure as rassophore took place. Peter was named Parthenius, and the other novice Plato. The brethren, apparently mistaking the names came to call Peter Plato, and his friend Parthenius. The father superior did not object and explained to the puzzled Peter that such, seemingly, was the will of God.
One day a monk came to the newly tonsured Plato and asked, "Do you serve Elder Nicodemus, who was godfather at your tonsure?" "No," said Plato. "You are supposed to serve your elder, brother. Bring firewood to his cell, light a fire when necessary, fetch water, sweep the floor and carry out various other jobs." Thanking him for his counsel, Plato went to Elder

Nicodemus. After having prayed he entered the cell and fell to the feet of the elder and asked forgiveness for his ignorance. The elder said: "It is enough that you do the common daily obedience, after all, I do not need anything. Thanks to God, Who gives me strength, for now I can serve myself." Plato bowed and left the cell. But when the monk learned that Plato had not received any instructions from the elder he advised him: "Go to him again, and ask him to give you a cell prayer rule." Plato thanked him for his instruction and went back to the elder. "You, brother, are trained in reading and writing," said the old man. "The Lord will make you understand, which prayer rule you should carry out in your cell." A week later Elder Nicodemus left the monastery. Remembering that time, Païssy subsequently wrote: "Thus I was left like a stray sheep without a shepherd and mentor. And nowhere did I have the possibility of living in obedience to some Father, though, as I see it, my soul from my youth was quite easily inclined to obedience, but I did not receive such a divine gift through my unworthiness."

The quiet life of Plato in the Medvedovsky monastery was disturbed by a sudden persecution of the peaceful cloister by the local authorities. Things reached the point where an official representative came to draw up an inventory of all church property. Then he locked and sealed the doors of the church. When the church had remained closed for a month, the monks began to leave the monastery.

Plato once again began to think about moving to Moldavia, but he did not dare go alone to those territories. At this time, the monk who had been giving advice to Plato - his name was Martyr, and also Father Crescene were preparing to go to the Kiev Monastery of the Caves. Plato decided to travel along with them. The month of December set in. The winter happened to be cold and snowy. The young monk suffered severely from the cold. With God's help, they reached the city of Vasilkov, the birthplace of venerable Joseph of the Caves. There they stayed for six weeks, waiting for admission to cross over to left-bank Ukraine.

Finally, the pilgrims safely reached Kiev and sent a petition to Archimandrite Timothy Shcherbatsky[6], the Father Superior of the Kiev Monastery of the Caves (Lavra), asking him to accept them in the ranks of the brethren. They received the blessing to live in the Near Caves before a final decision was made. When they had passed a probationary period, they were invited to the counsel of the Lavra, where they were given obedience and a cell. Father Martyr was appointed assistant of the econom[7], Father Crescene received the blessing to sing in the choir, and monk Plato was appointed to a special obedience.

It turned out that Father Superior Timothy, and the late Archpriest John Velichkovsky, the father of monk Plato had studied together for some time at the theological school of Kiev. In memory of their sincere friendship, Father Timothy assigned Plato to the printing press to learn from father Macarius how to engrave icons on copperplates. Plato's cell was located in the economo row which he shared with a hieromonk and a hierodeacon. Every day, except on Sundays and on holidays, he worked in the printing shop. Diligently he attended the services: the early Liturgy, the vespers and the matins. Soon the leader of the right choir gave him obedience: singing and reading the Services of the Hours and of the canons.

When Lent started, Plato went to the Far Caves to hieroschemamonk[8] John, nicknamed Kmit[9]. He was the general confessor of the Lavra. The young monk confessed to him. After reading the prayer of absolution, the confessor said: "I realize that God has preserved you from lapsing into heavy sins. If you spend your life in a hermitage under the guidance of an experienced elder, then maybe you will keep body and soul from big sins until your very death. But I am afraid that in our monastery, situated in the middle of the world, with us sinners, your soul might be harmed. If you want salvation, I give you this advice: do not drink any intoxicating beverages. Then with God's help you will manage to save your soul. Can you, my son, indeed follow my instruction?" Plato told him that from childhood he had not drunk anything intoxicating, and that it was contrary to his very nature. But he promised to follow this spiritual advice with all his power.

Many of the brethren came to love monk Plato for the severity of his spiritual life. In particular the head of the print shop, hieromonk Benjamin, felt affection for him and cared about him.

Chapter 3. Reminder about a Promise made in his Youth

Plato lived in the monastery for over a year, and all that time the thought did not even occur to him to leave that holy place. Once the assistant blacksmith called him and suddenly said: "O my beloved brother, I regret so much that soon you will leave our holy monastery and that you will go to another place that God has appointed for you." The young monk replied, "Believe me, most honourable father, I don't even think of leaving the monastery, on the contrary I hope with God's help to stay here to the end of my days." And again he heard: "Let it be known to you, brother, that in the very near future, you will fulfil my words by your deeds. Then you'll believe that I told you the truth." Plato did not contradict the ascetic again. He bowed and went out of his cell, struck by the prediction.

A few days later he was visited by Alexis, one of his closest friends from his studies at the Kiev academy. They greeted each other, began to talk and Alexis said, "My beloved father, and my friend with whom I am unanimous in the Lord, do you remember our decision neither to be tonsured nor to live in such cloisters where there is all kinds of wealth and bodily comfort, but to retreat from the world and be tonsured by a hermit and to be with him in holy obedience to the end of our days, and when in need of food and clothing to earn it with our own labour. Now I see that you have broken our covenant, and instead of living in the silence of the desert, you returned to your homeland and settled in this rich cloister." The young monk replied: "Yes, there was a vow. But when I left the world and my fatherland, none of you went with me. Our friend Demetrius did not listen to my advice and stayed with his mother. During my travels, when I found ascetics who were dear to my heart and beseeched them to take me in obedience, I received refusals. And there was not one of you near me who could help me. So I returned to my fatherland, and settled in this monastery." Then he said resolutely: "Here I have found perfect peace for my soul, and I intend to stay in this holy monastery." Alexis suddenly asked: "What if I suggested that you come with me to wander and live together in a desert monastery, what you would say to that?" The young monk probably heard in this question a secret, cherished aspiration of his soul, because he replied, "Oh, my beloved friend, if you're decided on this, I would go with you right now." The friends tearfully prayed to God asking for His help and blessings.

Alone in his cell, Plato couldn't help being surprised at the sudden change in his intentions and such a rapid fulfilment of the predictions of the blacksmith.

The friends began to gather their things for the road. They found people who undertook to help them. With great difficulties they reached the border of Moldawallachia[10] and there an unpleasant event happened. Alexis's cousin, had somehow learned of the intentions of the friends, and stopped them. He had brought along with him men who took Alexis by force to his mother in Kiev, paying no attention to his desperate pleading and crying.

Monk Plato, with a suffering soul, but otherwise quite problem-free, arrived at the Matroninsky monastery of the Life-giving Trinity at the beginning of Lent 1742, and he was cordially received by the founder and Father Superior of the monastery schemamonk Ignatius.

In the monastery there temporarily dwelled an ascetic of high spiritual life, hieroschemamonk Michael. The young monk greatly appreciated the spiritual talks with the experienced ascetic, but he remembered at the same time that Christian life should not be limited to conversations even if they are the most elevated and sincere. Christ expects of us that our wishes and decisions turn into actual deeds. The righteous young man tried to implement immediately in his own life everything he heard from the ascetic to the measure of his strength. Thus through this experience, he acquired more and more spiritual skill.

Learning that the permanent residence of the ascetic was in Moldawallachia, monk Plato told him that he yearned already for a long time to go there. Hieroschemamonk Michael praised his intention and advised him to go to Treysteny, the hermitage of his disciple, hieromonk Dometius.

At the end of Lent 1743 after the glorious Feast of Christ's Resurrection, monk Plato together with three other monks left for Moldawallachia. Bidding farewell to the ascetic the young monk began to ardently ask about his spiritual friend Alexis, for whom he had prayed, and he hoped that the inscrutable ways of the Lord would lead him to this monastery. He requested that hieroschemamonk Michael would take him in as a spiritual son and take him afterwards to the hermitage. The ascetic promised to fulfil this request.

After many days of travel the brethren had safely crossed the Ukraine and, having crossed the river Dniester by boat, they entered the territory of Moldawallachia. Finally, they reached the Treysteny hermitage of Saint Nicholas, and were received by the Father Superior hieromonk Dometius. In the hermitage twelve monks lived coenobitically and fifteen remained in seclusion not far from the monastery, each in his own cell. Here for the first time the young monk heard church services, performed strictly according to the Athos rule, "with great reverence and fear of God."

In this monastery a special spiritual atmosphere reigned. Here lived, for example, schemamonk Prothero, a native of the town of Reshetylivka, near Poltava. In the world he had been a jeweller. The schemamonk loved to receive and entertain wandering monks, and, just as he fed the pilgrims, he also fed all the birds that were flying about. The birds gathered in his cell. When he came to the window and opened it, they fearlessly flew into his cell, pecking out of his hands, and Father Prothero took them in his hands and stroked them. When he went to the church, the birds followed him, and sang in different voices. When the ascetic entered the church, they sat on the trees waiting for him, and afterwards they would escort him back to his cell.

Monk Plato thanked God for having vouchsafed him to live, pray and work in a monastery of such purity and simplicity. Because of his feebleness, he was given an obedience that did not require a great physical effort. When the head of the hermitage, along with the brethren all went to the forest to gather and prepare firewood, Plato was assigned to cook dinner. Learning that he did not know how to cook, they left with him a brother, so that he would teach Plato. He showed the young monk what to do, and went off to help the brethren. Plato however, in his inexperience and nervousness, could not cope with this obedience. He wanted to move the pot from the fire, but overturned it, burning his hands and spilling everything on the floor. With sighs and tears he put the pot back on the fire. The brethren returned from the woods and saw that dinner wasn't ready. They were upset, and prepared food themselves. This happened several times, and one can only wonder at the patience of the brethren.

Gradually, the young monk learned to cook, and then he was assigned to bake bread. As usual, one of the brethren showed him what to do and then he went off to his obedience. Plato however did not succeed in properly kneading the dough. At noon the brother came back and he had to knead the dough himself. But with this his difficulties did not end. Plato had heated the oven so much, that the bread immediately burnt. He took the blackened bread out of the oven and waited in fear for the return of the brethren. When he saw them, he fell on his knees out of shame and tearfully asked for forgiveness. "All this I tell about myself with the aim of preventing those arriving at our monastery to lose heart when they see their lack of experience, and to remind them that with God's help and with diligence they can achieve success in any work," Elder Païssy wrote later in his autobiographical notes, because he did not want to hide his mistakes and to try to present himself in a favourable light.

Soon, Plato heard joyous news: hieroschemamonk Michael had returned to Treysteny, with Plato's old friend, Alexis, whom the Lord had led along inscrutable ways to the Matroninsky Monastery. In the hermitage Alexis diligently served in his obedience. Plato was amazed at the strength and adroitness with which his friend was doing heavy work. During the Dormition fast Elder Michael tonsured Alexis a rassophore. Their life was spent in prayer and obedience. Plato had been zealously attending the church services, especially on Sundays. But once he had slept so soundly that he did not hear the ringing of the church bells, and it was only on arriving at the church, that he realized that he was late for the morning service. Greatly ashamed, he decided not to enter the church, but to return to his cell, lamenting and grieving about the temptation that had occurred. He could still have made it to the beginning of the Liturgy, but such a strong shame came over him that he left his cell, sat on the ground, and wept inconsolably. The Liturgy was over. The brethren gathered for the meal. Elder Michael, the hieromonk Dometius and all the brethren were surprised by the absence of Plato and they sent monk Athanasius to fetch him. With difficulty he found the crying Plato and he persuaded him to come for the meal. When he saw the monks sitting at the meal waiting for him, he trembled with shame and he fell to the ground sobbing inconsolably. He was told to sit down with them, but Plato could not eat anything because of his big shame and sorrow. When after the meal Elder Michael went to his cell, he addressed the brethren, especially the young, saying: "Do you see what zeal and what burning grief this young brother showed! Unintentionally he missed the prayer, and how he grieved, how bitterly he mourned and wept. You also pray to the Lord, that he may give you all the same zeal and burning grief for God!" Indeed, since then Plato no longer slept on a bed, but sitting on a bench.

In October schemamonk Onuphrius came to Treysteny from the Kyarnul Hermitage of the Archangel Michael, situated in the mountains, three days journey from there. He began to talk about the beauty of the place, about the clean air and water, the stillness and silence, which are favourable to a life of prayer. Plato had a great desire to go there. Sometimes in their early youth he and his friend Alexis had wanted to be in such a blessed place. Elder Michael blessed Plato and five young monks to move into this hermitage, but Alexis did not go with them, preferring to live his established life in Treysteny.

They walked through big forests, over high mountains and through deep valleys and on the third day they reached the Kyarnul Hermitage, where they were received with love by the Father Superior hieromonk Theodosius. The next morning each of them was lodged in his own cell. The monastic rule of this hermitage was like that on Mount Athos: the hermits lived alone in their own cells, praying and working. On Sundays and feast days the brethren gathered in the church to attend the service. On ending the Liturgy, during the meal and until the vespers they spent time in spiritual conversation and after the vespers they parted and went to their cells, where each completed his prayer rule.

Elder Onuphrius spent his time in prayer, reading, psalmody and manual work carving excellent wooden spoons, cups and saucers. Plato did not want to be idle and wanted to earn his daily bread, according to the commandment, with his own hands. So he made himself a little vegetable garden and planted some beans and onions, but there was not a good crop. Then he obtained the necessary tools for manufacturing spoons and began to learn that work, but soon dropped it because his lack of ability.

The brethren often came to Elder Onuphrius and listened to his stories about life in seclusion. The elder told them about the passions of the soul and the body, of the terrible mental and unceasing battle with demons... He said that the man-loving Christ is the only protection against them, that "those who prostrate themselves before Christ God in faith and love, with humility and with tears, will soon be given unspeakable comfort, peace and joy in the Lord, and burning love for God."

Listening to the words of Elder Onuphrius, the young monk started to burn more and more with love for God and a desire to become an anchorite. Through the force of his growing aspirations, he started to retreat regularly into the depths of the forest. There he would prostrate himself on the ground, with tears asking Christ God for help, and making vows. Thus he daily laid, like many of the holy fathers before, "a foundation for his amendment and spiritual ascension."

While at the Kyarnul Hermitage, monk Plato began to understand what are inner work and spiritual insight, what are true silence, temperance of the mind and inner attention, what is prayer of the heart, which is said by the mind while it is focused in the heart. Therefore, it was easy and joyful to undergo all sorts of hardships and extreme poverty, while in silence. Being among true ascetics who were in the possession of moral virtues, continually praying in their mind, focused in their heart and fulfilling the commandments of God, he kindled in himself a fiery zeal for spiritual feats and utter silence. This first stay of the ascetic in Moldawallachia lasted for about three years. He believed that these years were the best, the happiest time of his life as a hermit. There he had found the desired hermit's silence and experienced mentors of the spiritual life. However Plato once again decided to go wandering. What prompted him this time? The ascetic was troubled by talks that the elder considered him worthy of the priesthood, despite his young age. The young monk decided "not to take on such an awesome and responsible ministry, being aware of his unworthiness," and prepared to leave for Mount Athos. He visited all the elders who were living in silence, and with tears he asked them for forgiveness, for blessings and prayers, thanking them for their kindness to him, their fatherly love and spiritual guidance. The elders did not want to let Plato go and admonished him to stay. But, seeing his inexorability, calling him "a young elder," they said a prayer, and, entrusting him to the will of God, they released him in peace.

Chapter 4. Asceticism on Athos and the Instructions of Elder Basil

Since ancient times, Mount Athos has attracted Christian ascetics, and become a centre of spiritual enlightenment. In North-eastern Greece, amidst the azure waters of the Aegean Sea, there is a peninsula called Chalkidiki, which is covered with olive and pine groves. The unusual shape of the peninsula resembles a trident. One of the three projections is Mount Athos, 80 kilometres in length and about 12-20 km in width. This part of the peninsula is mountainous, pitted with innumerable rocky ravines. The top of Mount Athos is situated on the south side. It has a height of 2033 meters above sea level. Almost the entire mountain, with the exception of the cold peaks, is covered with abundant vegetation. Here grow lemons, oranges, pears, walnuts and chestnuts and vines take root well. The eastern slope especially is intensively cultivated. Mountain streams supply Athos with fresh water. The sea breeze tempers the torrid heat of summer. Snow falls rarely and doesn't last long.

In pagan antiquity the majestic mountain was known as Apolloniadu (after the temple of Apollo), and later there stood a temple of Zeus, which in Greek was called Athos. Church tradition tells us that the most holy Mother of God, after receiving the Grace of the Holy Spirit in tongues of fire went forth to preach Christianity with the apostles. As the lot fell to her to preach in the land of Iberia (now Georgia), she prepared to go there, but she received tidings from an angel, that her labour of apostleship was elsewhere. The ship, on which Mary and the Disciples of Christ headed for Cyprus, to Bishop Lazarus, got in a storm and was forced to moor at Athos. The pagan people accepted Mary and listened to her preaching, and they came to believe and were baptized. The most holy Mother of

God worked many miracles there before she set sail for Cyprus. She installed one of the disciples as a head and teacher there and said: "May this place be the lot given me by my Son and God." Then she blessed the people with the words: "May the grace of God be upon this place and upon those staying here with faith and reverence and those who observe the commandments of my Son and God. May the goods that are necessary for life on earth come to them with little work and in abundance, and the life of heaven be prepared for them and the Mercy of my Son on this place not diminish until the end of time. Indeed I'll be the patroness of this place and a faithful intercessor for this place before God." Since then, Athos is under the special patronage of the most holy Mother of God. At the top of the mountain is a church of the Transfiguration of the Lord.

In the XVIth century under the rule of the Ottomans, namely of Selim II, a difficult period began. There were uprisings against the Turkish rule: one in 1770 under the leadership of Daskalogiannis, another in 1821, a revolt blessed in the holy Lavra by archbishop Germanos. Parts of Greece only started to become independent in 1830.

In spite of these most difficult hindrances in the XVII-XVIIIth centuries, Athos became a place of Greek enlightenment, scholarship and publishing: at the Vatopedi monastery in the middle of the XVIIIth century, the Athonite academy (the Athonias) was founded, and at the Lavra a printing press was set up.

Monk Plato was 24 years old when he reached the holy Mount Athos in 1746. Travelling gave him a lot of physical suffering, and he had to first cross the Black Sea and then get to Mount Athos from Constantinople through the Bosporus Strait and the Sea of Marmara and across the Aegean Sea. But the Lord did not abandon the persistent monk. His companion was monk Triton. How often where they not struck by fear and how many disasters didn't happen to them during the sea voyage!

On the eve of the commemoration of venerable Athanasius the Athonite, July 4th, they reached the monastery founded by this saint. There was an eight hours' walk from there to the Pantocrator Monastery and not far from there lived monks of Slavic origin. From them the travellers were hoping to get advice and guidance as to how they could arrange their lives on Athos. The road to the monastery was hilly and rocky. It was hot. On the way they drank cold water, lay on cold stones. But the most dangerous was the fact that they travelled without a guide, they walked in places hazardous for one's health: in some places poisonous gas leaks from crevices in the mountains. The consequence of this is a serious illness: the so-called "fever of Athos". With difficulty they reached the Pantocrator Monastery. The brethren gladly received their compatriots. They assumed that their disease was connected to their sailing on the sea, and curing it would not be difficult. But when they realized that it was "Athos fever", they became distressed. What did they not do, to cure the poor wanderers! Hieromonk Triton could not be saved. The confessor of the monastery administered him the holy Mysteries, and on the third day he passed away. Plato was forced against his will to eat and drink much wine, which caused him to vomit a lot and to perspire, but that probably helped to oust the poison. By God's mercy, a few days passed and he recovered.

The young monk, fulfilling his cherished dream, began to search on Athos for a true spiritual guide, an idea he had cherished since his youth. But the venerable elders, who were at that time on Mount Athos, lived according to the ideals of hesychasm, in seclusion and obscurity, and sometimes they did not even know of the existence of one another. No one took Plato on as a disciple.

Hesychasm is prayerful silence. It is not simply peace of mind and life out of the world in a secluded spot. It is the focusing of one's whole being and life in the heart, to attain abidance in God as the only source of true peace. Saint Gregory Palamas, archbishop of Thessalonica, in the XIVth century, revived the practice of hesychasm. Reading the "Ancient Patericon", the sayings of Egyptian Christian ascetics, we can see that hesychasm is not a new doctrine. When Elder Arsenius asked the Lord how he could be saved, he heard a voice saying, "Arsenius, avoid talking, be quiet, dwell in solitude." That is in essence an encouragement to inner labour. According to venerable Simeon, who lived at the turn of the X-XIth centuries, God is light and He reposes in ineffable light. Therefore, he who reaches unity with God, communes with His eternal light and he himself becomes light. This is possible in faith and virtue, and hesychasm, prayerful silence, in his opinion, is the most perfect of virtues, while other virtues are just the way that leads to it.

Saint Gregory Palamas says about hesychasm, referring to the images of the Holy Scriptures: "He, who remains in prayerful silence, will hold Jesus' feet like the whore [from the Gospel], kiss them and pour spiritual tears over them. Like a bondmaid, whose eyes are fixed on the hands of her mistress to see any movement, he will look at the hands of the Lord his God, without taking his eyes off them. Like a bride, he will belong to Christ his God, he will lie down to sleep and stand up for the sake of eternal life. Like the Disciples of Christ on Mount Tabor, who saw His glory and heard the voice of the Father: "This is my beloved Son," he will fall prostrate, and say: "Lord, it is good for us to be here." He, who is prayerfully silent, will be like Moses on the top of Mount Sinai. He will be in solitude hidden from others in a cloud. If he will proceed thus, the Face of God will be clearly disclosed to him. And in the contemplation of God, and contemplated by God, listening to His voice, he first opens, in a mysterious way, the mystery of the Kingdom of God. Then he will give the law also to others, he will become illuminated and he will illuminate others with the light of knowledge, he will be shown mercy, and he will be merciful to others."

Insatiable hunger and thirst for God and the eternal Divine light is the main motive for the complete renunciation of the world. It is on such thirst, yearning, and ascetic labour that the life on holy Mount Athos is based.

In his ascetic narratives venerable Peter of Damascus, a XIIth century ascetic, testifies that this thirst is not the property only of monks or hermits, but is in the nature of all Christians. "That ascetic labour," he says, "is necessary for all Christians in one way or another. Without it the acquisition of spiritual knowledge and humility of mind is impossible. For those who seek it, the innermost secrets of the divine Scriptures and of all creation will be revealed." Without prayerful silence, said the holy father, we cannot be cleansed and we cannot get to know our own weakness and [to fight] devilish deceit. Without it, we cannot understand the power and the providence of God we read or sing about in God's words.

In our time, in the XXIst century, archimandrite Basil (Gondikakis)[11] writes that it is exactly in solitude that suddenly understanding comes "how unfounded the opinion of many people is, that those involved in practical activities and people devoted to contemplation are very different from each other." "Life's vocation is the same for all. And this vocation is love: the procession from the narrow darkness of selfishness to the promised land." "It is *not* so important that we succeed in what we plan, it *is* important however that the Holy Spirit creates in us and with us what He wants." True hesychasts "... are united by freedom of spirit. They are free of their own will to decide by themselves with sobriety and love either to live in the desert or to labour in the world. It is impossible for a physical separation to segregate them, or for a different way of life to change them essentially."

The ascetic Plato, who had left the world to go through the "school of the seclusion", did not find an elder. So he entrusted himself to Divine providence. He lived as a hermit in prayerful solitude. He led this life of asceticism for forty months, gaining spiritual strength and ascending to God in his heart. All the time he prayed with tears. He spent the nights reading the Holy Scriptures and the works of the holy Fathers. He borrowed books from the neighbouring Serbian and Bulgarian monasteries. The young hermit had a meal only every two days and this was only dry bread and water. He was satisfied with an old under rason and a patched top rason. A simple plank served as a bed. With such an ascetic life, he continually thanked God for having vouchsafed him in all to be an imitator of His poverty. Later he wrote: *"With my bodily weakness, I supplied in my needs by alms alone. And if the holy fathers of Slavic origin, who lived on the Holy Mountain, had not helped me, I could not have subsisted there. Many times I went barefoot in the winter... and thus I lived for up to four years. When I had to crawl either from the Lavra or from Chilandar to my poor cell carrying alms, or to bring firewood from the forest, or to do some other heavy work, then for two or three days I could only lie as if paralyzed."*

At the beginning of 1750 schemamonk Basil Polyanomerulsky[12] arrived on Athos. He was the spiritual guide of the ascetics with whom monk Plato had talked in Moldawallachia: hieroschemamonk Michael, hieromonk Dometius, schemamonk Onuphrius. Plato was not in direct obedience to Elder Basil, and never visited the Polyanomerulsky Hermitage. They met when Elder Basil visited his disciples in other hermitages, and talked with them about the monastic life, prompting the brethren to accomplish ascetic works and to daily read the patristic writings. Many of his teachings concerned prayer of the heart. He particularly stressed the "incorrectness of the opinion of those who think inner work is appropriate only for perfect people who have attained passionlessness and holiness. Those who think in this way restrict their prayer solely to an external performance of psalmody, the chanting of troparia and canons, not realizing that such external form of prayer is assigned to us by the holy fathers only as temporary because of the weakness and infancy of our minds, so that we will gradually improve and ascend to the level of inner work, and by no means we remain at mere external prayer."

Elder Basil sought to resolve the confusion and questions regarding the teaching of inner prayer. He thought it was incorrect that allegedly "first you need to purify the bodily senses well, so that you wouldn't sin through them, and only then start mental prayer." The elder said that this view is not consistent with the practice of hesychasts: "Friends! No one is against purifying the bodily senses, but if you separate purification from inner prayer, you'll get a lot of dissent. Because this way it looks as if you will never start with sobriety of the mind (inner prayer). Those who know mental prayer from experience do not separate one from the other (guarding the outer senses and learning mental prayer), but prescribe to learn them simultaneously and collaterally: to immerse the mind at the time of prayer into the heart and to tame the agitation of the senses, not allowing the mind to become involved with the senses. Doing this, they obtain a great silence in the mind and the heart and by controlling the mind they gradually learn not to succumb to carnal lust."

Elder Basil searched out Plato and stayed with him for a few days, sharing his solitary life in conversations and prayer. At the request of the young hermit the elder tonsured him into the mantle[13] with the name Païssy. At the time it was extremely useful for Plato to talk with the elder. The experienced schemamonk explained to him the danger of solitude for a beginning ascetic and advised him to choose a more peaceful and less dangerous path, namely, a coenobitic life with two or three brethren. "It is better to live together with a brother, thereby getting to know your own weaknesses and limitations and repenting and praying to the Lord about them, than living an isolated way of life and thereby feeding and covering up the vanity, self-importance and cunning which are in you," he said to the diligent ascetic. Païssy was 28 years old at the time. Despite his youth, because of his extraordinary perceptiveness and commitment to constant search he had been rather successful in the spiritual field by absorbing the experience of the ancient ascetics.

Three months after the tonsure of Païssy into the mantle monk Bessarion of Moldawallachia came to Athos. He was unable to find an experienced instructor in the spiritual life and in tears began to seek advice from monk Païssy. "Brother, you're forcing me to talk about sad things... How can I lead anyone on a path that I did not walk myself? I myself have to fight a hard battle against all the passions of my soul and my body, to overcome with the help of Christ lust and anger, to heal with humility of mind and prayer my soul from insanity and pride, to conquer voluptuousness, love of praise, love of money, and all the other evil passions... Someone who with humility and love can follow the Lord in all this and who will receive from Him the ministry to cure other souls will be able to show a disciple in practice all the commandments of Christ and all the virtues without deceiving him... *We* can only study day and night the divine writings of the Fathers and, consulting them, learn to carry out the commandments of God and to follow the example of our holy fathers," thus monk Païssy replied.

After hearing these words, Bessarion fell at Païssy's feet and began to tearfully beg him to accept him as a disciple. Païssy was embarrassed at that request. He himself had not noticed particular changes in himself and was unaware that he already had acquired some spiritual experience and therefore he did not think about instructing others. Only after much persuasion, did he agree to accept him, but not as a disciple, but as a friend and brother equal to himself. They decided to work together to find salvation, "showing each other God's will, the one to whom God will give greater understanding of the holy Scriptures revealing it to the other, encouraging each other to fulfil God's commandments, and all that is good, curtailing their own will and mind, obeying each other in all that is edifying, one at heart and with one desire in common, sharing all that is necessary for their daily existence." Thus Païssy started to follow the advice of Elder Basil and he began to live "with a like-minded brother in mutual love and obedience".

Four years passed. Monks started to join them. They insistently asked monk Païssy to accept them as disciples. The ascetic refused in extreme embarrassment. He persistently repeated: "To lead others is the lot of the perfect and passionless, and I am of feeble health, and possess all the passions, and therefore I am not worthy to teach you." But they relentlessly kept asking, and, finally, relying on God's providence, Païssy agreed to accept them.

The number of brethren increased. Soon they had to buy the Saint Constantine cell with a chapel. The first new brethren of the hermitage were from Moldawallachia, so the services took place in the Moldavian language. When Slavs began to arrive, the services were held in two languages: Moldavian and Slavonic. Twelve men gathered: seven Moldawallachians and five Slavs. Initially, their life was almost unbearable. Venerable Païssy later wrote about it in his notes: *"Before the onset of winter we had no place to live, as there were no cells, so we began to build five cells ourselves near the Saint Constantine chapel. Who can imagine the want we endured for four months. Nearly all winter we were building cells and carrying earth and stones! On Sundays or holidays, instead of resting, we had to run, nearly naked, to the monasteries for alms, in worn clothes, shivering from the cold. At that time, because of this great indigence after labouring so hard, many times the brethren came in at evening and dropped as if dead and fell asleep without having eaten. When we were in such need many times our rule was dropped, and instead of compline, I ordered only to read the Fiftieth Psalm ", and "the Creed", and then to bed. But even in those times we did not give up the matins, and according to our strength we read sometimes three kathismata, and sometimes more. Instead of the hours we read the Paraklesis to the most holy Mother of God[14], but sometimes we did read the Hours. And what more shall I say? Because of our extreme indigence we all would have run away if the most merciful Christ the Lord had not strengthened our humility, our patience and our love for God and one another by His grace..."*

Gradually, the difficulties were overcome. The number of brethren had been increasing all the time. Païssy received the permission and the blessing of the hegoumen of the Pantocrator monastery to buy another dilapidated church and the empty cell of the holy prophet Elijah, located right above the monastery, and proceeded to set up the Elijah hermitage. First the church was rebuilt, then - the courtyard wall. Against the wall sixteen cells were built for the brethren. All the buildings were made of stone. Besides that there was a refectory, a bakery, a kitchen and a guesthouse for pilgrims. A pipe-line was supplying the monastery with water. All the brethren were working at their obediences: they planted an orchard and a vineyard; they made different household utensils, and sold them. This allowed them to maintain the hermitage, to feed themselves, and also to receive and feed pilgrims. During the day Païssy laboured together with the others, but at night he copied the books of the holy Fathers. For sleep he had no more than three hours a day left.

According to church and monastic rule, in the monastery a priest is required to perform the Liturgy and a spiritual father for confession and instruction of the brethren. The brethren tried to persuade monk Païssy to accept the priesthood. He did not even want to hear about it. He said: "Because of this, I left Moldawallachia. The holy fathers wanted to force the priesthood on me there." The brethren answered: "When we confess to other confessors, we receive advice from them which is different to what you teach us. Our souls are dismayed by this because we do not know to whom to listen." Superiors of other monasteries, spiritual fathers on the Holy Mountain, joined the brethren in this request. They said to the inexorable ascetic: "How can you teach your brethren obedience and curtailment of their will, when you yourself refuse those asking you for something. It is because you love your own will and act only according to your own reasoning that you do not take into account the reasoning of those who are your senior in age and intellect. Isn't that disobedience?" Only then did monk Païssy overcome himself, obeyed, and with tears he said: "May the Will of God be done." He was ordained to the priesthood when 36 years old in 1758. Now that monk Païssy had become a priest and confessor of his humble monastery, even closer ties bound him to the brethren.
Word about the life of the ascetics of the Elijah hermitage spread on Mount Athos: the special way of life at the monastery, the reverential attitude of the brethren in church, the reading and chanting, the absence of needless talking, the grandeur of the services, and in the cells the handicrafts done in humility and silence. Many were surprised by the sincere peace among the brethren, their mutual love and cutting off of their will, their obedience to their superior, and on his side his fatherly mercy to his spiritual children. Hieromonk Païssy showed prudent moderation in satisfying corporal needs, but his attitude to the brethren weak in body and soul was

compassionate and loving. When monks came to meet the ascetic, they admired him and the great gifts God had given him. Many expressed a desire to stay in the hermitage. It soon became so crowded that the brethren lodged in twos and threes in a single cell. Apart from monks, also many pilgrims came to Father Païssy to hear his advice and receive his guidance. Sometimes it happened that there were so many pilgrims that he did not have time to talk to his brethren. Father Païssy came to be considered an experienced elder. Patriarch Seraphim, who stayed in the Pantocrator Monastery, called him to talk about spiritual subjects, faith, spiritual discourse, courageous asceticism, and the teaching of the God-bearing Fathers. They both burned spiritually, and sought to follow the Father's faith. Several times a year it happened this way: the Patriarch, the eldest fathers of the Pantocrator monastery, because of their love of Father Païssy invited him on Sundays or any other holiday to celebrate the Divine Liturgy with the monastery deacon in the main church of the monastery. Father Païssy celebrated in Greek, slowly and reverently, with the fear of God. Tears flowed down his cheeks continuously: in his whole life he could never serve a Liturgy without tears. Seeing this, the Patriarch, also in tears, said: "Glory to Thee, O Lord, glory to Thee!" Everyone saw him without reserve prostrated before God, transformed, and crying, barely able to utter the words. They were so touched and cried so much, that the monks, according to eyewitnesses, could not stay in the altar because of their tears. So they went out, marvelling at God's grace, and glorifying the Lord. This brings to mind the words of venerable Simeon the New Theologian! He wrote already in the Xth century: "There are few, and especially in our time, who can be good shepherds and especially few who can heal the reasonable souls. Some are still able to observe fasting and vigil, to maintain the appearance of piety. Many may also successfully teach with words, but those who achieve to cut off the passions and acquire the most important virtues by humility and perpetual tears, those are very few." "He, who wants to cut off the passions, will do this through crying, and he who wants to acquire the virtues, will acquire them through crying."

Father Païssy's monastery lived according to the coenobitic rules. In the course of several years, the number of monks increased to fifty. In May 1766 Païssy wrote to his old friend, priest Demetrius: *"You should know, my beloved friend, that the Holy Spirit through the holy fathers divided the monastic life in three ranks: the solitary sojourn of the recluse, living together with two or three like-minded brethren and coenobitic life."* He then expounded the basic features of these three ways of monastic life, the most detailed he described coenobitic life. Coenobitic life is created *"by the example of the Saviour and His apostles, starting with twelve brethren and it can grow to a numerous congregation, consisting of people even of different nationalities. The core principle of it is that all brethren gathered together in the Name of Christ, must be of one soul, one mind, one desire to work together for Christ by fulfilling His divine commandments, and by bearing each other's burdens, obeying one another in the fear of God and having a [spiritual] Father and mentor as head of their community. The brethren are obliged to obey their mentor like the Lord Himself by resolutely and completely severing and mortifying their own will and their own reasoning, i.e., not to oppose his precepts and teachings, if they [precepts and teaching] are in accordance with God's commandments and the teachings of the holy fathers.*

Communal life and holy obedience within communal life have been established on earth for the people by Christ the Saviour Himself." "The Son of God, in His love of Man and his mercy, renewed and restored this virtue in Himself: He was obedient to His heavenly Father even unto death, His death on the cross.

By His obedience, He healed our disobedience, and He opened to all true believers in Him, who obey His commandments, the doors of the Kingdom of Heaven. "
This divine obedience, being the root and foundation of the entire monastic life, is strongly connected to the coenobitic life, as the soul is connected to the body, and one cannot exist without the other. Obedience is the shortest ladder to heaven, having just one step - curtailing one's own will, and he who steps onto this ladder rapidly ascends to heaven. And he who falls away from obedience falls away from God and from the heavens, as our God-bearing fathers clearly testify."
It was not sufficient for Father Païssy solely to discourse about spiritual life. He gathered an active monastic community, inspired and imbued with one aspiration and a common cause. This was the fascination of his exploit. This was truly a new miracle on Athos. He introduced to the rule of the Elijah Hermitage a practice that was forgotten by many on Mount Athos: "spiritual work","inner prayer". The brethren laboured, studied the works of the holy fathers, cut off their will by obedience and humility and learned to unceasingly say the Jesus prayer.
Father Païssy and his monastery were inaccessible to the wiles of the devil, as it was protected by Divine grace. But through envy the enemy of the human race could take possession of the Father Superior of the Kapsokalivy Hermitage. Schemamonk Athanasius was older than Païssy. Envying Païssy's fame, he began to slander him, calling him deluded and a heretic. He also condemned sacred prayer of the heart, which Father Païssy taught his brethren. Knowing all this, the ascetic put up with it for a long time as if he had heard none of it. Then schemamonk Athanasius sent him a letter. It had in the beginning the appearance of a friendly admonition, but further it contained a lot of reproaches and philosophizing. The charges were as follows: Father Païssy violates

and reduces the rule of prayer established by the Church for the monks; he wrongly interprets the writings of Saint Gregory of the Sinai, he teaches an incorrect attitude towards the spiritual father, and he has come to resemble the Roman pope, who verbally acknowledges the commandments of the Church, but in his works he violates them. It was further stated that he has no humility, he trusts too much in the Greek manuscripts, he prefers philosophy to repentance and cry, he forbids cursing the heretics and he replaces the Church's rule with Jesus prayer. He urged elder Païssy to repent and not to violate the customs of the Holy Mountain.

After receiving this letter, Elder Païssy read it to his brethren and then showed it to his confessor. Along with his confessor, they went to the eldest fathers of the congregation. All of them were offended at examining this message, and they told Païssy to write an answer, exposing the misconceptions of schemamonk Athanasius and his untrue sophistications. If he will not repent, the spiritual fathers decided to denounce him before the synod of the whole of the Holy Mountain.

Elder Païssy wrote a 14 chapter answer to schemamonk Athanasius, in which he refuted all the charges. In his letter, he advises to read the works of the holy Fathers: *"I beg you, father, leave these vain and futile thoughts of yours... I praise you for your way of life, and I am pleased to see your exploits... But in addition to all of your works intelligence and reasoning are necessary, in order that all your work be not in vain. So if you want to find salvation and show your disciples the royal way then with all your soul cleave to reading books. That, together with questioning experienced spiritual fathers, will be a true teacher for you and your disciples, instructing you on the path of salvation. Otherwise, salvation is impossible."* Then he calls on Saint John Chrysostom and Basil the Great, and venerable Anastasius of the Sinai also to bear witness to the benefit of reading books. *"And do not tell me, Father, that [re-*

peatedly] reading one or two books is enough for the soul to be sufficiently instructed. After all, also a bee does not gather honey from one or two, but from many flowers. In that way in one of the books by the holy Fathers one would find instructions about faith or about correct thinking, in another book about silence and prayer, in again some other about obedience and humility and patience, in still another about self-reproach and love for God and one's neighbour, In short, from many patristic books a person learns the life according to the Gospel."

To explain the shortening of his rule of prayer, Elder Païssy tells about the extreme difficulties of the beginning of his life on Athos, when at times he lay for two or three days as if limp, not being able to carry out the rule. *"All this I confessed to my spiritual father and other aged confessors... Indeed, my spiritual father supported me. He said: "No, my child, do not leave the Holy Mountain. Stay there where God has summoned you, and bear His yoke for a little while. And keep your rule to the measure of your strength. Just always thank God, and God will not forsake you. God will value your thanksgiving in feebleness and need as a replacement for all rules. And following his advice, I kept my minor rule, and I lived, rejoicing and giving thanks to God in my infirmity..."*

The reply of humble Païssy made a strong impression on Athanasius, who realized that it was he who had been exposed to temptation. He repented and came to the ascetic and asked his forgiveness. Elder Païssy joyfully received him, and in a brotherly conversation revealed to him with love, what is the rule of life of the monks of the Elijah Hermitage. Since then, peace was established between them.

Elder Paissy on Mount Athos

In his understanding of monastic life Elder Païssy relied fully on the teaching of the Holy Fathers. He wrote: *"I was left like a sheep without a shepherd, so I began to wander here and there, trying to find for my soul something beneficial, to find rest and to be able to understand. And I did not find it except with the blessed Elders Basil and Michael, from whom I received monastic instructions and great spiritual benefit. But I could not stay for fear of being ordained to the priesthood.*[15] *So I reached at last the quiet and undisturbed haven of the Holy Mountain, hoping to receive some comfort for my soul at least here. Not having found the desired guidance for my soul, I settled for some time in a solitary cell, and, relying on the will of God, I began to read little by little in the patristic books... It was as if I saw in a mirror, with what I ought to begin my poor monastic life! I realized of how great a grace of God I was deprived by not living in obedience to an experienced spiritual mentor, and not receiving from anyone any instruction on this subject! I realized that my poor so-called silence was not my limit! Being at a loss what to do and whom to commit myself to in obedience, I grieved and wept like a child crying about his deceased mother."* An unquenchable thirst for patristic teaching on the spiritual life and inner work was expressed in this sincere contrition of the heart.

On the Holy Mountain the ascetic obtained a saving source in the books of the ancient God-wise Fathers who captured the true experience of communion with God in their works. From his youth his soul had aspired to patristic wisdom, from the moment he first touched these books full of revealed and concealed wisdom. But it was on Mount Athos, that he began to study the patristic texts with a special zeal, on another level of comprehension now, probably largely based on his own spiritual experience.

Comparing Slavonic manuscripts from various periods, Father Païssy discovered in the texts many inaccuracies and inconsistencies which bewildered him. Trying to make the necessary amendments to the Slavonic manuscripts using other

Slavonic manuscripts he soon realized that that was useless. "I lost all hope of finding in the Slavonic translations the correct and true sense of what was in the?? Greek originals," said the ascetic. To correct the translations of the ancient Slavonic patristic works he needed the Greek originals.

In the years Father Païssy spent on Mount Athos, he managed to learn not only the everyday Greek language, but also "Hellenic-Greek", as it was then called. It was the language in which the books of the ancient Fathers were written. One of the brethren, named Macarius, knew the language well. They started looking for these books in order to correct the Slavonic translations. Judging from the stories of Father Païssy, the search continued for a long time. *"Inquiring of knowledgeable people, of experienced and aged clergy and pious monks... from all I got the same answer that they not only did not know these books, but even that they had not heard of the names of their compilers... How could that be in such a holy place, where many great saints had lived?!... And that deeply saddened me. However, I did not lose hope in God and prayed to Him, that He as Almighty, Who knows each one's fate, would help me find the desired treasure. And the merciful God did not reject my ardent prayer...*

One day I was walking with two brethren... We suddenly had the desire to go to the Hermitage of Saint Basil the Great that was founded recently by monks from Caesarea in Cappadocia. We went partly to worship, and partly to explore the place, as we had not yet been in this hermitage ... A monk saw us and cordially invited us to his cell, and he went to cook something for us to eat... Looking at the table, standing at the window, I noticed an open book lying on it, which the monk, obviously, was copying... It was a book by Saint Peter of Damascus. Unspeakable joy engulfed my soul! I felt as if I had found a heavenly treasure on earth! When the monk came into the room, I asked him how such a precious book had ended up in his cell.

He told me that he had another book of the same saint. To my further questions the monk answered that in their hermitage besides these books one could furthermore find books by Saint Anthony the Great, Saint Gregory of Sinai, Saint Philotheus, Saint Hesychius, Saint Diadochos, Saint Thalassius, "A word on prayer" by Saint Simeon the New Theologian -, "A word on prayer" by the holy monk Nicephorus -, Saint Isaiah, and other similar books... These books were written in the purest Hellenic-Greek, which now, except for scientists, hardly any Greek understands... When the monks of this hermitage, were still in their homeland in Caesarea in Cappadocia, they heard about these books, and when they came to the holy mountain... they tracked them down in different monasteries. They copied them, read them and to the best of their ability they tried to follow their teachings... I started to zealously ask the brother to copy these books for me, promising to pay him any kind of price for his labour. The monk, already burdened with copying, refused, but he took me to another monk, who also worked at copying. I began to zealously ask also this brother to copy books for me, promising to give him triple the price. He, seeing my ardent desire to have the books, refused the triple payment, and promised me to copy some part of the books for the usual price, as much as he would be able to do..."

Thus, Father Païssy finally found the treasure, which he had sought for so long, and he could begin to correct the Slavonic translations according to the ancient Greek originals. This happened two years before he had to leave Athos and return to Moldawallachia. The monk, who undertook to copy the books for him, managed within this time only to do part of the promised books. Father Païssy received these works as a great sacred object, and as a gift of God and he took them with him to Moldawallachia to make use of them there, both to check the Slavonic translations and for his own translation of them from the Greek language.

Meanwhile, the number of brethren living in the Elijah Hermitage grew and already exceeded fifty. More and more disciples applied to him. In vain the elder pointed at the lack of space and material poverty. Patriarch Seraphim and the fathers superior of the Athos monasteries advised him to move to the more spacious Simonopetra monastery. That monastery was vacant. The brethren had left it because of a large debt to the Turkish officials[16].
Father Païssy ventured to petition the synod of the Holy Mountain. He was allowed to move into Simonopetra. He relocated, taking with him half of the brethren. They lived for just three months in the new place. When the Turkish authorities found out that monks lived in the monastery they demanded the payment of the old debt, and collected 700 leva[17]. Father Païssy hurried to leave Simonopetra and return to the Elijah Hermitage.
This situation forced Father Païssy to seek a new place of residence. On Athos there was not such a place. After much deliberation, Elder Païssy and the brethren decided to move to Moldawallachia. It is quite possible that they preliminarily negotiated with the spiritual and secular authorities there and received their permission. No doubt they already knew there about Father Païssy, and besides, his former spiritual ties had been preserved. In addition, some of the Elijah Hermitage monks were born there. There his coenobitic fraternity would be able to live and grow without any worries.
The seventeen years of works of Father Païssy on Athos had not passed unnoticed by the Athonites. The Elijah Hermitage that was founded by the elder became the foundation of the current improved Saint Elijah Hermitage, and his teaching has found its continuation in the life and work of the Athonite zealots.

Chapter 5. Wondrous is God in His Saints

"A "word" in the monastic language is a "spoken and true" thought, coming from the heart of the hermit as inspired by the Holy Spirit, and the questioner accepts it as a fruit of grace, without analyzing it with his own mind, and this word of the spiritual father is of the utmost necessity for his life."
Metropolitan Hierotheos (Vlachos)

In 1763, after a seventeen-year stay on the holy mountain, Elder Païssy and 64 monks left Athos and found refuge in Bukovina, near Dragomirna in the Holy Spirit Monastery, given them by the Moldavian metropolitan.
The brethren set sail for Constantinople on two ships. On one was Elder Païssy with the Slavs, on the other Father Bessarion with the Moldavians. They safely reached Constantinople, and then Galata. In Moldawallachia the community was temporarily housed in the Varzareshti Hermitage.
When they had settled a bit, Father Païssy went to the city Iasi to visit metropolitan Gabriel and was graciously received. Their spiritual conversation brought joy to them both. Metropolitan Gabriel blessed Father Païssy to live with his brethren in Dragomirna, in a monastery with a church, consecrated in honour of the Descent of the Holy Spirit upon the apostles. The metropolitan sent a letter to the Bishop of Radoutsy who was responsible for that monastery, so that he would hand over the monastery to Father Païssy and cooperate in every way. The local governor Gregory Callimachus freed the monastery from all possible tributes by a special charter. Seeing such a warm welcome and care, the ascetic thanked the Lord for His inscrutable good ways. He was sincerely glad that the powerful people of this world treated the monks from Athos with love and compassion.

Moldawallachia was in the XVIIIth century the refuge of those craving for the monastic life from all the neighbouring countries. The number of monasteries in Russia was significantly reduced due to a government policy that was carried out at that time and in Ukraine the orthodox was persecuted by the Uniate Catholics.

The Dragomirna monastery of the Holy Spirit is situated near the town of Sochava and the village of Itcani, which borders Bucovina and Moldavia in a valley of the Carpathian Mountains. On the outside it is a powerful fortress with walls and towers. It served as a refuge for the inhabitants of the city of Sochava when there was an attack of Zaporozhe Cossacks and Tartar hordes. The date of the foundation of the monastery and the name of its founder are unknown. The general opinion is that it was founded in 1602 by the Bishop of Radoutsy called Anastasius (Krimka). But at the end of the XVIIIth century two letters patent[18] of the Moldavian governor Peter VII the Lame were found, dated March 28 and October 21, 1584. These letters gave Dragomirna the everlasting possession of the arable land near the village of Kostin in the Sochava District. Consequently, the monastery already existed in the XVIth century. Perhaps Bishop Anastasius (Krimka) had restored and improved it.

The church of the Descent of the Holy Spirit upon the Apostles was built in 1602. In one of the towers above the monastery gates, there was erected a church of St. Nicholas. In the monastery garden they had built a church in honour of the holy prophets Enoch, Elijah and apostle John the Theologian. In 1763 the monastery was in a pitiful state. There were only five cells and the refectory had no roof. In the church a few liturgical books were found. As far as the farm was concerned, in the barnyard there were altogether six bullocks. However, the monastery covered a vast area, it was located in a quiet scenic place, and it was quite possible to gradually improve it. Elder Païssy and his community were all inspired and delighted with the new location.

Soon the monastery began to receive generous donations from many benefactors who wished to assist the monks. The pious governor Gregory Callimachus constructed two rows of new cells and an archondarik[19]. The boyars followed the example of the governor: one donated working cattle, another cows and sheep; others sent grapes, wine, wheat, and some - shoes and clothes. This general sympathy and generous help deeply touched the elder and the brethren. With tears of joy, they thanked God in prayer.

Elder Païssy soon presented the Moldavian metropolitan and the synod information about his monastic community and its rule.

"(1). Our first and foremost rule, which is always observed by us: none of the brethren may in any way own or call his own any movable or immovable property, nor the slightest thing, but all will be owned in common...

The father superior should see to every brother's need in food, clothing and so on. He should, as a father caring for his children, give each what is necessary... From this foundation sincere love for God and neighbour, meekness, humility, peace, concord and curtailment of will of the coenobite brethren will grow.

Obediences are carried out by the brethren... not for glory, honour and bodily peace and not for any other human concerns, but only for their own salvation. And through this they will be united heart and soul, and worldly envy, hatred, pride, enmity and any other malice will have no place among them...

(2). The second rule, on which, as we think, all monastic life depends, is to acquire obedience. That is, to spit on and throw out all one's own will and reasoning and arbitrariness, and to zealously try to fulfil the will and reasoning and the commandments of one's father, when they are consonant with holy Scripture, and to serve to the utmost the brethren, as if they were not people, but the Lord Himself, with fear of God and with humility.

(3). What should the father superior be like? He must be learned in the Holy Scriptures and the teachings of the Holy Spirit-bearing fathers, and not add anything of his own to their testimonies to the brethren: neither doctrines, nor commandments, but often instruct and reveal God's will. He must be guided by Scripture in the appointment of obediences, remembering that the Word of God is for him and the brethren the instructor and guide to salvation. He should be an example of humble wisdom and live with the monks in agreement, union and spiritual love. He should not start or do any kind of undertaking by himself without advice, but he should gather the brethren who are most skilful in spiritual reasoning and with their advice, and after searching the Scriptures, start to act. If something serious happens, it must be announced to the whole congregation. So the whole congregation should be gathered and under its general authority and consideration action should be undertaken. There will then l be peace and concord between the brethren, and an unbreakable bond of love.

(4). The general Rule for Divine services: vespers, compline, midnight office, matins, hours and Divine Liturgy. On all feasts of the Lord, of the Mother of God, and of the great saints there will also be all-night vigils with readings. On the smaller holidays also the polyeleos and praise with readings. On other days the whole church rule and the order of service according to the rule on the Holy Mountain of Athos, should always steadfastly be carried out in our monastery without haste and on time.

During the service, living and deceased founders and benefactors of the holy monastery should be commemorated according to the rule and the statutes of the holy Church.

The superior and all the brethren should always wear the habit and klobuks fitting to their rank, as specified by church rule. This should never be given up, except in case of illness or work of obedience. And if any of the brethren doesn't attend the church, the father superior must interrogate him in front of all the brethren at mealtime. If he does not acknowledge his fault the father superior must give him a fitting canon[20] to read during the meal, or order him to abstain from food for the day, and he must bring him to spiritual understanding verbally as he usually does.

(5). Every day at table the father superior and the monks should observe the general church statutes on what is allowed to be eaten and what not. At the table the brethren have to wear habit and klobuk according to their rank, and remain in complete silence and fear of God, giving heed to the readings. There should be readings every day from the lives of the saints and patristic and didactic books according to the church rule.

On Sundays, the Lord's great feasts and celebrated saints' days, and if possible, every day, there must by all means be a Panagia[21]. Meals in our community should be according to the order of the Holy Mountain. And in no way may neither the father superior nor the brethren eat in their cells, except in case of illness or extreme old age. All should have the same food, only those with a diseased stomach may have special food that is good for them. However, even they should eat in the refectory, and not in their cell.

(6). The brethren should stay in their cell in the fear of God according to the tradition of the holy fathers. They should of all possible works prefer prayer of the heart, which is God's love and a source of all virtues. It is performed in the heart by the mind, as many God-bearing fathers taught. Apart from prayer there should be psalmody, moderate reading of the Old and New Testament, and of didactic patristic books. In addition, one should whether in the cell or anywhere else and in all matters remember death and one's sins, the last Judgment and eternal torment, and the kingdom of heaven, do handwork or art designated by the father superior. One should in no way be idle, for idleness leads to all kinds of evil. Untimely leaving the cell and irrelevant conversations should be avoided as poison. So which Fathers teach about prayer of the heart Saint John Chrysostom, Saint Callistus II, patriarch of Constantinople, Saint Simeon, metropolitan of Thessalonica, Saint Diadochos, bishop of Photiki, Saint Hesychius of Jerusalem, Saint Nilus of Sinai, Saint John Climacus, Saint Maximus the Confessor, Saint Peter of Damascus, Saint Simeon the New Theologian, Saint Gregory of Sinai - all these and other holy fathers teach about prayer of the heart.

(7). The father superior ought to test the humility and obedience, and the curtailment of the will and reason in all matters, which is the ladder that leads the novices to the kingdom of heaven. He has to send the brethren to work in the kitchen, in the bakery, with the cellarer, in the refectory and to do all other obediences within the monastery. The brethren should look at Christ, the founder of all feats, Who has shown a heroic deed of obedience and humility. They should not refuse the seemingly lowest kind of obedience. They should believe it will lead to the kingdom of heaven if they serve the brethren with humility and fear of God, as if they [the brethren] were not people but the Lord Himself.

(8). The father superior must love all brethren equally. He must carefully observe whether the brethren love each other truly and not feignedly. Their love should be the sign of their discipleship of Christ. Particular love for a certain person and special friendship which are based on preferences are a source of envy and ruinous to true love, and should be eradicated in all possible ways.

The father superior should endure all weakness and falls of his children long-sufferingly, in the hope of correcting them, and of their true repentance. He should correct them in a spirit of meekness, admonishing only as far as is useful [for the soul].

Those who live by their own arbitrariness, who follow their own will and reasoning, who reject the beneficial yoke of obedience and by this cause harm to others, should in no case be tolerated. After sufficient instruction and admonition, in private, with two or three brethren, and before the council they should be separated and expelled from the community. Even if there are many tears and regrets and malady[22] of the soul, this will prevent others to become infected with their pernicious disease. Those who come to their senses and convert to repentance should be received again with joy, and they should be shown all kinds of mercy and compassion and their transgressions should be forgiven, rejoicing with all the brethren at their conversion.

(9). The father superior must appoint a skilled brother to manage the land and the monastery serfs and all external monastery affairs. This brother must be able to govern these external affairs without violating the commandments of God and without ruining his soul. Being free the father superior can with greater convenience take care of the spiritual salvation of the brethren and of all beneficial church and coenobitic discipline.

Similarly, an assistant is needed for the spiritual care of the brethren: a brother with a trained intellect, who during the absences of the father superior could be left with the brethren for their spiritual nourishment. When he has the intention of being absent, the father superior should collect the whole community in the church with a bell, venerate the holy icons, let the priest say the prayer for the journey and announce his intention to the community. He has to ask humbly for their prayers to God, so that he may return in good health and safely. And, having asked for forgiveness from all, give his blessing, and depart on his way.

When he returns from a journey, he should not go straight to his cell, but having gathered together the brethren, first go to the church and having given thanks to God, thank also the brethren for their prayers.

(10). About accepting a brother in the monastery. A brother is driven by God from the world into monasticism. The father superior should first try him and explain to him from the Scriptures the power of monastic coenobitic life, obedience to God, and ultimate curtailment of one's will and reason. If he detects a true and unfeigned desire of monasticism and divine zeal, then in front of the whole community, he should again reveal to him the power of coenobitic life and obedience. And he should not immediately tonsure him a monk, but after a set time, established by rules: some should be kept in worldly clothes for three years, others for six months, depending on the fruits of obedience and curtailment of their will.

Some should be tonsured a rassophore, and some into the mantle. With this they are joined to the fraternity. The father superior keeps a brother for an established period of trial, and if he still does not perceive in him true obedience and curtailment of the will after three years, he should not be tonsured but sent back into the world, so that he will not be a temptation to the coenobium.

(11). If the newly-arrived brother brings with him any property to the monastery, then the father superior must keep that property intact in the monastery's treasure house until the tonsure. Only after tonsure it may be used for the general needs of the monastery, because if the brother wants to return in the world or go to another monastery, then all the property he brought with him must be returned to him in its entirety, so that neither the brother, nor the monastery will be embarrassed in any way.

(12). Inside the monastery a ward should be arranged where brethren who are taken ill can be cared for and receive special food, drink, and the necessary rest. A trained brother should be placed there, able to serve them in a spiritual mentality, and if someone in the monastery knows the art of medicine even partly, he also must be placed there.

(13). The father superior has to take care that the monks know various crafts, and especially those necessary for the coenobitic life. The brethren should be assigned to those crafts and those who have no skill should be trained, so that the needs of the whole monastery can be met without trouble, and there is no necessity to go out into the world.

(14). Two guest houses must be arranged: one inside the monastery for spiritual and worldly persons coming to the monastery, and the other outside the monastery. Let the people who come to the monastery find appeasement for themselves in the monastery while their cattle must be kept outside the monastery. The father superior should appoint two skilful brethren to supervise these guest houses.

The father superior should have a spiritual love for the brethren and show the same love to all coming to the monastery, to the poor, the sick, and those who have nowhere to lay their head. He should receive with love one in the guest house, another in the hospital according to their needs and take care as far as is within his powers of their bodily needs.

All these and other coenobitic statutes we upheld on the holy Mount Athos according to our strength and here we do the same as much as possible. Only the guest houses are not ready yet and we do not have enough cells for the brethren, so we live crowded. But we hope that God will give us everything we need, so that every brother will have his own separate little cell as a quiet and untumultuous haven after the labours

according to the church rules and the various obediences, for his inner work and physical feats, as well as rest.
(15). We implore Your Eminence, that the entrance to the monastery will be forbidden for the female sex except in case of extreme necessity in times of war and flight, and also, that the hermitage of saints Enoch, Elijah and John the Theologian will never be separated from the monastery. Let brethren from the monastery be assigned there by the father superior and the whole community. And let them to get all they need to get for life from the community.) Let there by no means be pilgrim-monks and those who have private property. And if the Synod so decides, let them fulfil the church rules and the Divine Liturgy according to the decision of the Synod for the commemoration of benefactors and founders.
(16). The monastery serfs will be moved to the village and a church with a married priest will be arranged for them, so that the peace of the monastery not be disturbed.
(17). About the order of election of hegoumen. Let there not be another father superior until the death of the former one. A superior should not be sent from elsewhere but he should be chosen unanimously from the community by the whole of it according to the advice of the dying father superior and with the blessing of his eminence the metropolitan. He should surpass all in spiritual intelligence, knowledge of sacred Scripture and of the coenobitic statutes, and also in obedience, curtailment of his will, in love, meekness, humility and all the virtues and he should be capable of giving the brethren a good example in word and deed, and have the venerable rank of priest.
Since our community is divided into three dialects, he must be familiar with three languages: Greek, Slavonic and Moldavian, or at least two - Slavonic and Moldavian. However if a superior should be sent from elsewhere, rather than be chosen by the brethren, how can he manage a herd of Christ's

sheep if he has not in actual fact achieved perfect obedience and curtailment of his will and reason, if he has not endured reproach and dishonour in the coenobitic life, if he does not know the power of Scripture and the coenobitic rules, if he still has private property and if he accepts this nomination not to put his own soul at stake for the community, but only to have rest for his soul and to enlarge his property? And how will the brethren submit to such a teacher? If something like that should happen, then nothing other will result from this, than the absolute and complete dissipation of the community and the devastation of its coenobitic life. Can really no one be found in the whole monastery able to lead the community to salvation by word and deed and example? But even then, if by extreme necessity someone is sent from outside the monastery he must only be installed with the voluntary assent of all the brethren, after having promised God in front of all the brethren not to have or acquire any property for himself alone and to own everything with the brethren. Only under such conditions will there not be a total collapse of the coenobium."

This rule, in which industry and contemplative life are harmoniously combined, was approved and adopted. Thus, venerable Païssy put an end to the tragic dispute between the "possessors" and the "non-possessors"[23]. This painful conflict gradually led to the extinction of eldership [spiritual direction] in the XVth century, and subsequently influenced the whole spiritual life of Russia. Elder Païssy put the emphasis on the state of the soul of each monk. He shared with his disciples his experience of prayer, after the evening meal he led discussions with the brethren, read and commented the patristic writings.

The divine services became the basis of spiritual life and they were performed strictly according to the rite of the Holy Mountain. Singing with two choirs was established: in Slavonic - on the right, in Moldavian - on the left. The rule of the coenobium was strictly adhered to as before in Greece. All were appointed an obedience with the blessing of the father superior, who himself shared the general labours. All worked at their obedience willingly and diligently, faithfully, for the Lord's sake and according to their strength. What new did Elder Païssy bring to monastic life? What attracted disciples to him? Why did his undertaking achieve so much with further spiritual waves across Moldawallachia, Russia, Ukraine, and so strongly influence the formation of monastic life? Probably because the elder had a rare gift, the ability to create a unique spiritual attunement in the monastery, which he himself defined as "of one soul, one heart".

When there was work in the crop fields the brethren spent a few days away from the monastery. With them was a priest who had the Holy Gifts with him. If necessary, a doctor was called. Often, Elder Païssy came to them during the harvest of grain and spent two or three days with them in the field. He truly enjoyed their diligence and held edifying talks with them. When the elder left, the brethren lovingly accompanied him, asked for his blessing and prayers, kissed his hand and returned to work, glad to have seen their spiritual father, and to have listened to his instructions.

When the elder could not personally visit the reapers, he sent them a written greeting. *"Protect yourself from envy. Where there is envy, there is no spirit of God. Restrain your tongue, so that it does not speak empty words. Who spares his tongue spares his soul from sorrow. The tongue can bring life and death. Seniors need to teach the younger and the inexperienced. In all there should be humility, kindness and love. It is necessary to strengthen in oneself the fear of God, the memory of death and eternal damnation. Every day you need to confess your thoughts... Repeat the Jesus prayer constantly. Bring to God a pure, undefiled, fragrant sacrifice, according to your*

Christian vows. Bring your work and your sweat, as a burning offer. Endure the burning sun as the martyrs." The elder prayed to the Lord to keep away from those who labour all spiritual and bodily evil and to protect them from all the wiles of the devil. Such letters were imbued with love and care and encouraged and inspired the brethren, and made their hard and tedious work easy and pleasurable.

With special attention Elder Païssy observed the life of the brethren in their cells. Every evening they had to talk to their confessors, disclosing all their thoughts. If a misunderstanding occurred among the brethren, they had to make their peace the same day according to the words of the Scripture: "let not the sun go down upon your wrath" (Eph. 4:26). And if any of the brethren was so hardened that he could not make peace, the elder would ban him, forbidding him even to stand on the threshold of the church, and tell him to pray the Our Father, "until he resigned himself".

Obedience brings fruit, it grows into love. Love is verified by the sincerity of the heart of the brother who lives in obedience. The aim of renouncing one's own will is to soften the heart, release it for the love of God and one's neighbour. This is a victory over anger: "Let no one be angry with his brother, and indeed not with anyone at all, because then he is angry with Christ. I heard once how someone was angry with his brother and I told him: "Brother, is there no fear in you? Are you not terrified that you are committing such a thing...? Don't you know you're angry with Jesus?" He replied: "But I'm not angry at Jesus, God forbid, but only at a brother." "Tell me then, you, who are angry with your brethren, do you believe the holy Gospel? What does Christ say in the Gospel? Verily I say unto you, Inasmuch as ye have done it unto one of the least of these my brethren, ye have done it unto me (Mt. 25:40). Therefore whosoever is angry with his brother does not keep his anger back from Christ. That means that someone like that does not in the least believe in the holy Gospel. So let him take care he will not be condemned along with the infidels!"

There was one brother, who rebelled against the elder. In anger he denounced him for reprimanding him. Venerable Païssy answered him: "My dear brother, anger is the opposite to life according to the Gospel, and anyone who hates another, falls into ruin. If the Gospel orders to love even your enemies, how could I hate my spiritual son? As for my reprimands, o, if the Lord would give you that kind of anger! I take on the state of mind of each of the brethren: with one I have to be angry, with others, by contrast, I must be tearful, sometimes in this way and sometimes in another, by these means and by those means I can be of use. But I never become a victim of passion... In my youth I made a vow to God: "Lord, if I'm ever going to judge my brother, even if I saw with my own eyes how he has sinned, let the earth swallow me." I put a seal on my lips, so that I could not ever say to anyone a single word, and I closed my ears and eyes, and with the grace of Christ, I kept this vow for my whole life up to the moment I began to live with brethren. Then, although against my will, I became your judge. The brethren themselves have allowed me to speak to them and to mind their business for their benefit. Before, I did not say anything."

When the elder held a talk, it was to develop morals and manners, understanding and obedience in a brother. With the more intelligent he used to talk about lofty subjects, explaining his words with the holy Scripture, and he amazed and consoled a brother to such a degree that that brother was ready, because of the spiritual joy he felt, to regard all the glory, joy and sorrow of the world as nothing. With the more simple brethren the elder talked more plainly, giving examples from their craft or obedience, and in his own words he brought them to the point they felt they were ready to reproach themselves and repent.

Elder Païssy told the brethren, that when he sees his spiritual children labouring fervently and jealous about keeping the commandments of God, humbly carrying out holy obediences, then he feels such an indescribable joy, that a greater joy he does not wish to have even in the kingdom of heaven. When however he sees that they are not rejoicing in the commandments of the Lord and despising holy obedience, then his soul is embraced by such sorrow, a greater sorrow there cannot be even in hell.

In the cell Païssy advised to indulge in moderate reading of the Holy Scripture, in psalmody and in the prayer of the heart. One day there came to the elder a brother, who said that thoughts are bothering him a lot. Païssy smiled and said, "Why are you so silly? Do as I do: With you I am arguing all day and with another I am crying, with others I am rejoicing and doing other things. When I chase you all out of your cells, then together with you I chase out all thoughts. Then I pick up a book and I hear nothing, as if I am in the silent desert of Jordan."

From the first days in Bukovina, venerable Païssy introduced a custom, which had a beneficial effect. In winter, when the brethren were free from work in the fields, and all had gathered in the monastery, the elder held talks with them. From the beginning of the Christmas fast[24] until Lazarus Saturday, every night, except on Sundays and holidays, they gathered in the refectory and lit candles. The elder began to read from the works of the holy fathers, explaining them and illustrating them with examples from the Old and New Testament. "Brothers and fathers, with contrite hearts we ought to take care[25] of our salvation, as the divine fathers teach. Saint John of the Ladder says: "Even if we lead an exalted life, but if we don't acquire a grieving heart, then all this is pretence and in vain." And Gregory of Sinai says: "Contrition and humility, and the labour of obedience according to one's strength, with an innocent heart, these all usually lead on the right path of truth." And again Saint Gregory: "All bodily and spiritual work, if it does not comprise labour of the heart, will never bring fruit to the one who is carrying it out, for the kingdom of God is attained by effort, and those applying effort achieve it, as the Lord said. For even if someone is labouring for many years, but without inner suffering and unconcerned about performing works of penance with a zealous heart, he may be as one foreign to purity and who does not commune with the Holy Spirit... He, who works with negligence and laziness, even if he seems to be working a lot, will work in vain, because he who does not walk the path of inner pain, lapses into harmful concerns because of depression and his mind darkens." The same is also said by Simeon the New Theologian: "He, who does not imitate the Passion of Christ through repentance, tears and humility, obedience and patience, and especially through poverty and tribulations, defamation and outrage, and who never partakes of His shameful death, he cannot be co-partaker of His spiritual Resurrection, and he cannot obtain the grace of the Holy Spirit." Divine Paul says: "For to be carnally minded is death; but to be spiritually minded is life and peace... Therefore, brethren, we are debtors, not to the flesh, to live after the flesh. For if ye live after the flesh, ye shall die: but if ye through the Spirit do mortify the deeds of the body, ye shall live...The Spirit itself beareth witness with our spirit, that we are the children of God: And if children, then heirs; heirs of God, and joint-heirs with Christ; if so be that we suffer with him, that we may be also glorified together." (Rom. 8: 6,12,13,16,17)

Citing the words of the holy Fathers, Elder Païssy tearfully urged the brethren to keep the commandments of Christ and to gain a contrite and humble heart. All of his teachings, all his concerns, all the affection of his heart were aimed at ensuring that the brethren did not spend the time given them by the Lord for repentance fruitlessly and in negligence. He urged them to work hard studying works by the holy Fathers.

Elder Paissy in Moldavia

"Let none of you say that it is impossible to cry ...and repent every day. First of all, you need with strong faith and warm love to come to the Lord and to renounce decisively this world with all its beauties and delights, to renounce your will and your reasoning and to be poor in spirit and body. And then, with the grace of Christ, a holy zeal will be kindled in perfect souls. In the course of time and to the extent of one's labour tears and weeping are given, and a little hope to console the soul. Hunger and thirst for truth will appear, that is, an ardent zeal to act in everything according to His commandments, to achieve humility and patience, mercy and love for all - all these are fruits of the Spirit. A zeal will appear to endure the weaknesses of your neighbour, to give your life for your brother, to stand firm in all sorts of temptations, insults, vilification and reproaches, to forgive each other with all your heart all grief, to love your enemies, to bless those that curse you, to do good to them that hate you, to pray for them who offend you, as Christ expects from us. In addition to all that, to courageously endure with gratitude all sorts of bodily affliction, infirmity, fierce and bitter illnesses, temporary sufferings for the sake of the eternal salvation of your soul. In that way, you will become "children of Christ's bride chamber" (Mt. 9:15), perfected to the extent of your spiritual age. And if you remain firm in such works, then also your community will remain standing, as long as it pleases the Lord. But if you turn away from guarding yourselves and from reading patristic books, you will fall away from the world of Christ and His love and the fulfilment of His commandments, and among you will dwell disorder, vanity, difficulties, confusion, hesitation and despair, grumbling and mutual condemnation. Because of the multiplication of all this, the love of many will turn cold, and perhaps even the love of all. And then your community will be ruined, first psychologically and then physically."

In Dragomirna Elder Païssy continued the work that he did throughout his whole later life – the translation of patristic works into the Slavonic language. All activity of study, correction and translation of patristic texts, especially hesychastic[26] instructions, was oriented on the needs of the monastic community. Evening conversations became especially important in the life of the brethren, because during those conversations the problems of inner spiritual struggle were placed on the foundation of the exegesis[27] of the Holy Scripture and the teachings of the holy Fathers. "Read so as to act," said the elder.

The ascetic worked at night, correcting the Slavonic translations of patristic works. Older translations were to a large extent inaccurate and sometimes distorted the true meaning of the text, so the elder used the Greek originals to correct existing books, but also to make new translations. His diligence was incomprehensible. There was almost no time for sleep left.

He wrote to Archimandrite Theodosius: *"When we moved into the holy Dragomirna monastery, I started to think in every possible direction about how I should proceed with the correction of the Slavonic patristic books, and even better, with a new translation of the patristic writings from the ancient Greek language. However, I encountered many obstacles related to this cause. The first obstacle was that the translator of the books should definitely be quite a knowledgeable man, and not only in grammar, spelling, and in the characteristics of both languages, but also in the higher sciences such as rhetoric and philosophy, and he should also be skilled in Theology itself. Even though I spent in my youth four years at the Kiev colleges, I learned there only a part of the Latin grammar. My further studies were interrupted by my desire of monasticism. Moreover, that little information that I had obtained at that time, I had almost lost over the years, so I was afraid and trembled to start so great a work of correction or translation of patristic books with such weak knowledge. The second obstacle was my lack of proficiency in orthography. Who dares to write sacred books if he is not proficient in spelling? That is, in my opinion, somebody who blasphemes with his hand as a result of his lack of proficiency, even though with his heart he believes in the truth and with his lips he confesses unto salvation. That is why I was horrified to begin such a great work, being at that time as yet not adept at spelling. The third obstacle was the fact that I did not have the necessary dictionaries. To translate books without dictionaries is like engaging in a profession, not having the necessary tools.*

The fourth obstacle was that I knew at the time very little ancient Greek words because I did not really know this language at all. The fifth obstacle was that the ancient Greek language surpasses all other languages of the world in wisdom, beauty, depth, abundance and richness of expressions. Even born Greeks, who are perfectly educated, can barely perceive its depth. How could I, being so unknowledgeable, dare to embark on the work of correction or translation of books from such a wise language? The sixth obstacle was the fact that I also insufficiently knew our own glorious Slavonic language, which, in my opinion, surpasses many languages for its beauty, depth and abundance of figures of speech, and closest of all approaches the ancient Greek language. Taking into account all these factors, as well as the fact that I was too burdened with countless spiritual and corporeal, and internal and external cares of different kinds, I almost lost hope of ever starting... this work. But I saw that in our fraternity many were starving for God's Word. That completely exhausted the souls of the brethren as well as my own soul. I put all my hope on the Lord Who makes the blind see and I decided to finally start the work, but with great caution and relying on the prayers of the brethren...

Elder Paissy in his cell

I began my work as follows: Due to the lack of dictionaries, as well as my inexperience, I took as a guiding thread for myself the translation of some patristic books from ancient Greek into

Moldavian, made by our beloved brothers hieromonk Macarius and Hilarion Daskalov, people trained and experienced in the translation of books. Part of this translation was done by Brother Macarius when he was still on the holy Mount Athos, and another part in Dragomirna. Also Father Hilarion worked on his translation in our fraternity. For all these reasons I assumed their translation to be correct and started to correct the Slavonic books, guided by their translation and following the ancient Greek original. In this way, I corrected the following Patristic books: Hesychius, Diadochos, Macarius, Philotheus, Nilus's "On prayer", Thalassius, Gregory of Sinai, Simeon the New Theologian's "A word on attention and prayer", Cassian the Roman's "About eight thoughts" and others. I held on to the Moldavian translation like a blind man to a fence. In that way I completed the first correction of those books.

After some time, when little by little I began to come to a better knowledge of my work, I noticed many mistakes in my first corrections. Then I corrected some of these books for the second time. After some more time, when I noticed new inaccuracies, I corrected them for the third time. Nevertheless, some books were left only with a first correction, because I did not have time to correct them for a second time. It must, however, be said that the books I repeatedly corrected were far from absolute perfection, as the ancient Greek books themselves, which were copied for us on Mount Athos, were in many places incorrect.

While correcting old Slavonic books and while I still did not even have a single vocabulary at my disposal, I nevertheless re-translated a second book with writings from the same ancient Greek books. They were writings of the saints Anthony the Great, Isaiah the Hermit and Peter of Damascus. But these translations contain so many mistakes as a result of my inability at the time that even thinking about that makes me afraid. It is in no way possible to properly make corrections if the right ancient Greek books are missing. At that time, I also translated the book of Saint Theodore the Studite from ordinary Greek, due to dire need of it. But up to the present time I still haven't had the honour of seeing it in ancient Greek. However, in this translation there are also many errors for the same reasons. The ancient Slavonic translation of the book of Saint Isaac the Syrian I corrected during a whole year, first checking it with the ancient Greek printed text, then with the Moldavian translation. But to my regret I see that this book is far from perfect and that I'll have to work anew on its correction, if only the Lord in his mercy will extend my life and give me the necessary eyesight, because I am already almost blind."

In the first years of his stay in Dragomirna Elder Païssy had come to the defence of the Jesus prayer, i.e., staying in the heart in prayer near Christ, as the chief means of overcoming evil thoughts and achieving purity of heart. In the Ukraine, in the Moshensky Mountains, there appeared a certain monk who denied prayer of the heart as a heresy and spiritual deception. This monk acquired such an influence among his brethren, that some after listening to his speeches gathered the patristic books that taught about prayer of the heart and sunk them in the river by tying stones to them. Hearing of this, Elder Païssy wrote a 6 chapter essay about prayer of the heart, which he also sent to the misguided monks. He also took pains to warn his own brethren about the proliferating attacks on prayer of the heart.

"The rumour has reached me," he wrote, *"that some persons of the monastic rank dare to blaspheme the divine Jesus prayer, which is the solemn performance of a religious rite with the mind in the heart. They base themselves merely on the sand of flimsy reasoning. They are instigated to do that, I dare say, by the enemy, in order to discredit this divine work and to cloud this spiritual sun by the blindness of their minds. I was concerned that someone listening to their fables would not fall for*

a similar blasphemy and sin before God by cursing the teaching of so many God-bearing fathers about this divine prayer. Also I was not able to calmly listen to the impudent words about this immaculate inner work. And I became persuaded by the intensifying requests of adherents of this prayer as well. I called upon my sweetest Lord Jesus and decided to write a few words about the divine Jesus prayer based on the teachings of the holy Fathers. This essay is a refutation of the false reasoning of the empty talkers, a confirmation for the God-chosen flock assembled in our monastery and a solid, unwavering and indubitable approbation of the prayer of the heart." This is followed by a presentation of the teaching of the Jesus prayer in six chapters. Bishop Ignatius Bryanchaninov[28] would in the next century react positively to this writing and other works of venerable Païssy Velichkovsky. He noted that they "set forth the teaching of the Jesus prayer, which befits our times very much". It "is an undeceiving representation of the practice of the Jesus prayer." Namely "such a practice... befits all Christians in general, those who live in monasteries as well as those living in the world."

In 1768 began the Russian-Turkish war. Residents hid in the woods out of fear. They looked for shelter in monasteries to escape from the Turks and Tatars. The Dragomirna Monastery was the most powerful fortress among the Moldavian monasteries, and was located in a barely passable forest in the Carpathian Mountains. In the first week of Advent the territory of the monastery was filled with rich and poor, adults and children. So much so that to pass through the crowd was difficult. All fled in fear and in a hurry, so the majority of the people had neither warm clothes nor shoes on their feet.

It was a harsh snowy winter. The elder, seeing the dreadful distress of the people, tried by all means to alleviate their plight. He gave half of the monastery to the people in need and moved all the brethren to the other part by putting three, four or five people in one cell. The refectory, a large and warm place, he gave to the weak, to the unfortunate women and children. The cellarer, the baker and the cook were ordered to give food to all who just arrived and were in need. Some people took raw supplies and prepared their food themselves, while others received cooked meals and bread like the brethren. They were baking and cooking continuously to feed everyone. "Really," writes schemamonk Mitrofan, "all those people stayed in and around of the monastery for about two weeks. Then they dispersed in all directions. But the boyars remained in the monastery for more than a year."

The war lasted for six long years. In addition, in 1771 God allowed other disasters to happen: pestilence, crop failures, and famine. Only in 1774 was the peace signed between Russia and Turkey. The brethren of the monastery were able to pick up their former life.

After the war, the Austrian empress Maria Theresa demanded part of Moldavia from the Turkish rulers. This had been promised to her for her help in the war against Russia. This part for the Austrians included, against the wishes of the Moldavians, the land of Bukovina. The Dragomirna monastery was located in this region.

Elder Païssy foresaw that from the side of the new authorities oppression would follow, which could lead to the ruin of the monastery. The whole fraternity realized the imminent danger. At this time, he received a letter from the father superior of the Secu monastery in Moldavia. It was an invitation to move and live in his monastery. The elder was glad of this invitation. He wrote to the Moldavian prince and the metropolitan letters of complaint saying that he could not remain under the rule of the Austrians. He asked permission to move with the brethren to the Secu (Beheading) Monastery dedicated to Saint John the Baptist near the little town of Secul. The Great-Prince as well as the metropolitan felt sympathy for the fate of Elder Païssy and his fraternity. In writing they officially approved their move to the Secu monastery.

After having received permission, the elder began to prepare for the journey. Fearing trouble and hindrances from the side of the Austrians, he made all his preparations in secret. First, he inconspicuously moved all church furnishings to Secul and after that he told the brethren they should pack their things for the road. At that time there were about 350 monks. They all expressed their willingness to go with their father superior. But the elder did not immediately move everyone to the other monastery. He left 150 monks in Dragomirna and appointed two confessors. One of them was Moldavian, the other was a Slav. He appointed the first as head of the monastery, and the second as his helper. They began to prepare themselves for the journey. To conceal his intention from the Austrians, the elder pretended he had sent the brethren to obedience on some monastery land that was in the same direction as the road to Secul. Before leaving *he* went to the church and prayed there with hot tears, after which he gave peace and blessings to the remaining brethren who were crying. First he headed for the place where the brethren who had already left expected him. He told the Austrian border guards that he was going to the monastery mill and so he crossed the border without difficulties. Near the monastery mill he met up with the brethren. They walked for more than a month, and on October 14, 1775 they safely reached Secul.

Monk Parthenius left us the following description of the Secu Monastery: "The monastery is in the Carpathian Mountains... The road there goes through a gorge between mountains so high that the sun cannot be seen. The monastery is located in a quiet and silent place, surrounded by high mountains up to the clouds and dark impenetrable forests, so that in winter the sun shines but a little, and there is never any wind, but there is always a great silence. Behind the monastery there runs a small river... Indeed, here the entire vain secular world with all its temptations is hidden from the eyes and ears."

In the XVIth century in this place was the hermitage of Father Zosimas. He came with his disciples, presumably from the Neamts monastery. These ascetics built a wooden church of Saint John the Baptist and a few cells. The local population quickly heard about the hermits. Benefactors were found. In 1595 the boyar Nestor Ureche from Lower Moldavia and his wife Mitrofana built a stone church in the monastery. They were buried in this church. In the monastery a silken shroud embroidered in gold and silver, the work of princess Mitrofana, has been preserved.

Together with Elder Païssy 200 monks settled in the Secu Monastery, not counting the novices. All of them were accommodated in fourteen cells. In the meantime came the winter cold. The patient monks, hoping for God's help through the prayers of Father Païssy began to build cells for themselves, first in the towers of the monastery wall, attaching them on the outside to the walls like swallows' nests; and then also outside the monastery, and in the woods. The work on the improvement of the monastery lasted for three years.

Little by little the brethren who had remained in Dragomirna began to join them. And new monks also came. The road to the monastery was difficult and so the monks were not so often visited by people of the world. Nevertheless, those wishing to become acquainted with monastic life came, despite the obstacles.

Venerable Païssy fulfilled the word of the Gospel: "Him that cometh to me I will in no wise cast out." (Jn. 6:37) and received all. According to the custom that had already taken root in Dragomirna, he spent the evenings conversing with the brethren in the refectory. He alternated the talks in this way: one evening they were in the Slavonic language, the other in Moldavian. He relied on almighty God's providence, and exhorted the brethren also to stand all want and crowded cells for the sake of the peace and silence in Secul and to thank the Lord for having vouchsafed them to bear the cross of poverty and shortage.

In the spring of 1779 the Moldawallachian ruler Constantine Mourousis sent charitable help to Secul and a letter to the Father Superior Elder Païssy, asking him to report all the needs of the monastery. The elder replied with a letter of gratitude and asked him to allocate 500 leva for the construction of workshops for a tailor, a shoemaker, a weaver, as well as classrooms for Greek lessons.

The ruler received the petition and addressed himself to the Senate with the question: "How should I see the Secu Monastery where Elder Païssy and his brethren reside?" One senator, who had had the occasion to visit the monastery, said he thought Elder Païssy and the brethren stayed there "as if in confinement". "The monastery is crowded. The church is small and is not intended for such a large community. The location of the monastery makes it virtually inaccessible to people in need of advice from the elder. The road to the monastery passes through a narrow rocky gorge. During the rainy season it is flooded, and this creates new obstacles for the delivery of donations to the monastery." The ruler asked: "Isn't there in our land such a monastery, where the elder and the brethren would not be in any need and could give guidance to those in spiritual need?" The senators responded: "Throughout our country there is not a more spacious and comfortable monastery than Neamts which is located at a short distance from Secul." The ruler was very pleased with this answer and decided to write to Metropolitan Gabriel.

The metropolitan agreed to grant Elder Païssy and his brethren the Neamts Monastery. The ruler then proposed to the elder to move into this spacious and comfortable residence. When he received the order, and learned about the unexpected decree, the ascetic was quite upset. He did not want to leave the remote monastery which was far from worldly vanity. The Neamts Monastery was comfortable, but at the same time more accessible for visits from worldly people, so the elder feared that it would be more difficult for the monks to maintain a rigorous life of prayer. He paid heed to the fact that not all the monks had spiritual understanding, not all cared about the sobriety of their minds and unceasing prayer to a sufficient degree. He foresaw inevitable complications in the merging of the monks of the Secu and Neamts monasteries into a new community. In addition, the ascetic understood that he would not be able to restrict access to the monastery to worldly people, especially women. They would want to enter the Neamts Monastery to worship the miraculous image of the blessed Virgin as they were accustomed to. He was also conscious of his own feebleness. The elder did not want to take on new cares and concerns related to an inevitable increase in the number of brethren. He was also worried that in the new community he would not be able to continue their traditional evening talks with the brethren, to explain to them the depths of spiritual life with patristic books.

Venerable Païssy began to think how he could ask the ruler to reverse his decision and leave him in Secul. Meanwhile, the spiritual fathers of the Neamts Monastery came to see the elder. They humbly entreated him not to discomfort them and not to change their usual way of life. The words of the Neamts monks seriously wounded his gentle soul full of brotherly love. He wished them all only peace, benefit and salvation. The elder showed them the order of the ruler and said: "You see, holy fathers! This is the reason for this embarrassing situation and our and your grief. May Christ the Lord be my witness that I did not even have one thought to inflict this on you... and to upset your souls... You yourselves know that it was not our own plan to live in Secu. But its former hegoumen, Father Nifont of blessed memory, invited us... Only then we wrote to the authorities and we received what we asked for, a residential permit... How would I dare to inflict such a thing on you...? How could I look at your holy faces if my own conscience would be the judge and accuser for the offense I had caused you? How can I proceed to the throne of God to partake of the awesome and divine Mysteries, when there are people crying because of me and blaming me before the Lord? May it not be so, let it not be so! On the contrary, I will write to the ruler and tearfully beg him to leave us and you peacefully reside in our own monasteries. We have a deep peace here, by God's grace."

The monks of the Neamts Monastery were reassured by this conversation and returned to their dwelling place. The elder wrote a very lamenting petition to the ruler. How many touching words did he not use in the letter? How many compelling reasons did he not bring forward? Having written the petition, he sent two spiritual fathers of the monastery to the ruler. The elder pinned great hopes on one of them, Father Irinarch.

The ruler read the petition. The fathers told him about life in their monastery. With tears they dropped to his feet. They pleaded to leave the elder and the brethren in Secul without embarrassment and temptations. The ruler became thoughtful, and suddenly asked Father Irinarch a question: "Are you obedient to the elder?" He replied: "Certainly we must listen to him and obey him, and all the brethren, until our death. At our tonsure as monks we made a vow before God." And unexpectedly they heard these words: "The holy father expects you to obey. Would it not be fitting then that at least he also obeys us? Otherwise, if he is disobedient, what kind of an example does he give you?" Subsequently the ruler did not listen to any more pleading and answered the elder: "Carry out this obedience and go to Neamts without arguing."

The monks returned to the monastery with the letter from the ruler and handed it to Elder Païssy. When he saw the severe command he became distressed. An immeasurable sorrow came over him and enveloped his soul to such an extent that he could neither eat, nor drink, nor sleep. The brethren were in fear and in great confusion, worrying that the elder would die of inconsolable grief. The oldest of the spiritual fathers and the community gathered and went to him and tearfully begged him to stop grieving and recuperate by taking food. They said, "What good would it be, if you, father, should die prematurely, and we remain orphans without you? What should we do then? The ruler is such a benefactor to us, even not having conceded to our petition. Clearly, such is the Will of God, it is not proper to resist!"

Elder Païssy, seeing the tears and confusion of his spiritual children, prayed, sighed heavily and tearfully said softly: "Brethren, it will be crowded for us wherever we are." Then he got up, crossed himself, bowed to the icon of the immaculate Mother of God, and said: "May God's will be done! Let us go even if we don't really want to." After that, the elder ate a little.

Elder Païssy suffered greatly because he had not managed to convince the ruler to leave the Secu and Neamts brethren to "dwell peacefully in their residences," so he called three spiritual fathers and a few monks and blessed them to go to the Neamts Monastery to pass the order of the ruler. The brethren did so and returned.

Elder Païssy began to think how to divide the brethren. Some were blessed to go with him to Neamts, and others to remain in Secul. For the spiritual nourishment of the monks in Secul he appointed as confessor Father Hilarion. The elder went into the church, humbly prayed to the Lord, and venerated the holy icons. He comforted the brethren who were sad because of the impending separation: "Come to me with all your mental and physical afflictions without any restriction."

Having said farewell to the brethren who were staying in Secu, Elder Païssy left the church and set out for Neamts. Brethren surrounded his one-horse wagon like bees. They walked slowly, enjoying spiritual conversations. Some walked along to see the others off who were going to the Neamts Monastery. They arrived safely in the monastery on "the very eve of the feast of the Dormition of the immaculate Mother of God" in 1779.

When the elder and the brethren came close to the Neamts Monastery, they heard the sound of bells. Neamts brethren came out to meet them. Leading the way there were three hieromonks in phelonions, one of them was holding the Gospel and the other two each a holy cross. Behind them were two deacons with censers in their hands. Venerable Païssy kissed the Gospel, the crosses, and went through the monastery gates. The elder was preceded by the priests and deacons. The brethren accompanied him. They sang irmoses from the canon to the immaculate Mother of God. Entering the church, the elder kissed the icons and prayed assiduously to the miraculous icon of the Mother of God, entrusting himself and the community to her intercession, protection and care.

The church hierarchy of the Neamts community, and Hegoumen Joasaph and his assistant Hegoumen Varlaam, led Elder

Païssy to the place of the hegoumen. When the troparion and the kontakion had been sung, and the ektenia and the dismissal had been pronounced, the elder humbly said that he came to the monastery not of his own will and striving, but by the decision and order of the ruler and the metropolitan. He asked all to keep mutual peace and love. After leaving the church the elder went to the cell that was prepared for him and took a little rest. The brethren who had come with him settled with a few in each cell. Only the spiritual fathers had separate cells.

The elder could not sleep out of sorrow, despite the fact that in the last five days he had not had any sleep. It is only with difficulty that he went to church at the beginning of the all-night vigil, and he attended the divine service sitting, praying to the immaculate Mother of God that she comfort his soul. Once the vespers were completed matins started, and the Gospel was read, sleep began to overtake him. The elder went out and returned to his cell. He was exhausted and lay down on the bed, but he fell asleep only when it was already dawn. He slept two or three hours. When he woke up at last he felt relieved. His sorrow, by the prayers of the Mother of God, had left his heart.

After the Liturgy, Elder Païssy called the former leaders of the Neamts Monastery to him. In the conversation with the spiritual fathers that ensued he promised to take care of them until his death and in no way to oppress them. They were completely reconciled with him. A few years later these holy fathers were clothed in the schema, and having lived piously, they departed to the Lord.

Only a few of the Neamts monks left the monastery. The majority joined the common brotherhood. Out of the two communities a single one was formed. Peace and unanimity were established. The elder wrote to the ruler about the move to the Neamts monastery, the reconciliation of the two communities and he asked for help in the construction of new cells. The ruler thanked the elder for his obedience and promised to help. He drew up a deed stating that the direction of the Neamts Monastery was handed over to Elder Païssy. The Secu monastery was to remain under his direction too. The total number of monks was 700. The rule that was accepted in both monasteries was the same. The brethren of the Secu monastery frequented the elder, and once a year he spent several days there.

In a letter to the ruler the ascetic disclosed a bygone event of his life. As a young monk, still before his departure to Mount Athos, he had come to pray in Neamts before the miraculous icon of the Mother of God and was awarded, he said, " three times to hold this holy icon in his sinful hands." Then he was filled with love for this place, and, by God's inscrutable ways he was led here with his community.

According to Bishop Arsenius[29], the Neamts monastery has the same meaning for Moldavia as the Trinity Lavra of Saint Sergius and the Kiev Lavra of the Caves for Russia and Ukraine. For centuries it has been a source of Christian enlightenment in Moldavia. It produced many Moldavian hierarchs: bishops and metropolitans who defended the orthodox faith in difficult times. For the whole of society the monastery became a university of moral life, by giving examples of selfless devotion and faith through its monks. During severe trials, the internecine war between the kingdoms, conflicts with the Turks, Poles and Hungarians, during famine, fires and other national calamities, orthodox Moldavia was drawn to the monastery and found protection and spiritual help there.

The monastery is situated in picturesque surroundings. Where the small mountain stream Neamtsul comes out of the Carpathian canyons and breaks into an open valley, among high hills covered with a centuries-old pine forest, the walls and buildings of the monastery show up white. The monastery was founded at the end of the XIVth century. Under Metropolitan Joasaph three monks came to Moldavia: Sophronius, Pimen and Silvanus with their disciples. They came from the Tismana Monastery and were disciples of venerable Nicodim, the Pious[30]. The Moldavian ruler, in all likelihood governor Peter Muşat, built a small church for them in honour of the Ascension of the Lord. The first document which refers to the Monastery of Neamts dates from 1407. According to this record, the monastery received tenure of the village. The monastery was expanded and grew rich thanks to generous donations of Moldavian rulers and pious sponsors. The history of the early years of the monastery is also connected with the name of the famous preacher Metropolitan Gregory Tsamblak[31], who arrived in Moldavia to be hegoumen of the monastery until 1420. The monastery received its name in all probability from the citadel of the XII-XIIIth centuries, built not far from it by German crusader-knights. The ruins of the castle are visible on a high cliff.

A more spacious church of the Lord's Ascension was built in 1497 by the ruler Stefan the Great. An inscription above the entrance doors bears witness to this. At the beginning of the XVIIIth century hieromonk Pachomius was hegoumen in Neamts. After hearing about Metropolitan Demetrius of Rostov[32], a skilful preacher of God's word, Father Pachomius went in 1704 to Russia to see the ascetic. He was granted to talk with the metropolitan several times and he received from him a book, written by his own hand. When Father Pachomius returned to Neamts, he settled with a few monks in the wilderness and gave himself over to the work of prayer. At that place there is now the Pokrovsky Hermitage; it is located at a distance of an hour's walk from the Neamts monastery. In early 1707 the hermit was summoned from his seclusion and ordained bishop of the town Roman in the eparchy of Roman in Bucovina. After governing the eparchy for seven years the bishop withdrew to the Pokrovsky Hermitage again, and three years later he went to the Kiev Lavra of the Caves. There he departed to the Lord in 1724. In his will the bishop set forth the rule of the Pokrovsky Hermitage. Thus, already in the early XVIIIth century there was a live connection between the Neamts monastery in Moldavia, Great Rostov in Russia, and the Kiev Lavra of the Caves in Ukraine.

In one of the churches of the Neamts monastery a shroud is kept. It is a beautiful work, embroidered with gold and pearls on crimson velvet. According to the inscription embroidered on it, the shroud was donated to the Neamts monastery by a nun called Maria in 1741. According to legend, the nun Maria was in the world the great princess Maria Petrovna, daughter of Emperor Peter the Great. She took the veil in one of the convents of Moldavia.

In the sacristy of the monastery there was kept a large altar Gospel, which two deacons had to carry at the time of worship. The Gospel was donated by a monastery in Saint-Petersburg in 1764. The miraculous image of the Mother of God, the one before which venerable Païssy prayed, is the main object of worship in the Neamts Monastery. According to legend, the icon was given by the Byzantine emperor John Palaiologos to the Moldavian ruler Alexander the Good[33], and he in his turn gave the sacred object at the beginning of the XVth century to the Neamts Monastery.

Elder Païssy adopted the existing rule of the monastery. Most of all he paid attention to the order of worship. Reading and singing was done according to the long-standing tradition of the community in two languages: Moldavian and Slavonic. At matins, between kathismas, two sermons were read, one in the Slavonic, and the other in the Russian or Moldavian language. The akathist to the Mother of God on the Acathist Saturday[34] was read in Slavonic, in Moldavian and Greek. In everything a close connection with the Russian Church was maintained. At the dismissal Sts Anthony and Theodosius of the Caves, and other miracle-workers were commemorated. On September 21th a service to the hierarch Demetrius of Rostov was done, on May 3rd, the memory of venerable Theodosius of the Caves was celebrated, on July 10th of the venerable Anthony of the Caves, on July 11th of the most orthodox princess Olga, on July 15th of prince Vladimir.

With the offerings of the ruler new cells were built in the monastery, as well as hospitals and guest houses. Special attention was paid to the care for the sick, elderly and pilgrims in the monastery. The elder put sick monks in the hospital and entrusted Brother Honorius with their care. He asked the brethren, who nursed the sick to serve them as the Lord Himself. In the hospital and the guest houses cleanliness was observed, and there was always the smell of myrrh. They tried to give the patients the best food. The infirm, elderly monks glorified God and thanked Elder Païssy and his community for his mercy and care. Pilgrim monks also found shelter and could stay at the monastery: some for a week or two, but some for a month. Some asked to spend the winter, and the elder gave his blessing to do so. In the summer the pilgrims left. With the blessing of the elder they were all supplied with what was necessary and seen off. Men from the world suffering from various diseases, as well as those who had nowhere to live, were also received into the monastery. They remained in the monastery as long as they wanted, some even until death.

On the feast of the Beheading of Saint John the Baptist the elder went to the Secu monastery and remained there for nine days. After the feast he gathered the community for talks. One evening he gave instruction in the Slavonic language, and on the other in Moldavian. All the brethren were free to come to his cell for advice. To those who stayed in the hospital, and to those who themselves could not see him, the elder passed his blessing through Father Dositheus. Father Dositheus surpassed all other monks in his care for the sick, in his mercy and compassion, gentleness and humility, quietude and love. The main church feast of the Neamts Monastery was celebrated on the day of the Ascension of the Lord. For this feast a multitude of people gathered in the monastery: distinguished people and ordinary people, rich and poor, not only from Moldavia and Wallachia, but also from other countries. Elder Païssy tried to receive all pilgrims, according to Abraham's hospitability to strangers. During four days from morning till evening his cell door was open. He thanked all pilgrims for having taken the trouble to make the journey, and after blessing them, he invited them to go to the guest house or to cells that were prepared for them. In addition, the God- wise elder introduced on those days the following rule: he instructed the more experienced brethren to look after the less schooled in the spiritual life, so that they would not fall in any temptation.

Elder Païssy continued to closely and carefully follow the life of the community of the Neamts Monastery. However, despite all his care, it was difficult for him to neutralize the unfavourable circumstances of life in a large monastery. Schemamonk Mitrofan, eyewitness of the events, wrote: "Towards the end of the life of the elder the quality of our spiritual life went down quite clearly and irrevocably compared to our unanimous, peaceful and loving life in Dragomirna and Secu. The reasons of this: general talk, excesses, rebelliousness, no longer studying the divine and patristic writings, and consideration of only oneself. The elder foresaw it all and wept often and warned the brethren. He urged all not to abandon attentively reading the patristic writings, to steadily adhere to the narrow path of the Gospel and to avoid negligent, falsely peaceful lives... In Dragomirna and Secu in winter, every night, there were lectures by the elder, but in Neamts, they stopped, and so we had to make more use of books. Here the elder was more engaged in translations and corrections. The visits of distinguished persons of both sexes also were harmful for the brethren." One travelling monk asked Elder Païssy: "How, father, is the current life in Neamts as compared to that in Dragomirna?" The elder replied: "Every year it goes down, and to retain the same standard is impossible, even though I try. The reason for that is unrestricted admittance of women and abandoning the lectures to the brethren."

Elder Païssy saw a decline of spiritual life in the monastery. From his point of view, an Evangelical community is first and foremost a community of individuals, which grows in the spirit only with the growth of each member. "He preferred that the monastery would fall to ruins, or that other valuables would be lost, than that the soul of a single brother would be lost and fall into transgression," stated another witness, Isaac Daskala.

On the whole, from the point of view of pilgrims, even if they were monks or ascetics, the life of the community presented itself in quite a different light. This is evident from the stories of the Solovetsky hermit Theophanes, who had the occasion to live in the Neamts monastery for a while, and also to visit other Moldavian monasteries. He examined their location, studied their statutes and customs. Theophanes spoke with great respect about the life of the Neamts monks. "Their non-possession was total: there was nothing in the cells except icons, books and tools for handwork. The monks particularly distinguished themselves by their humility. They shunned pride and vanity. They did not know hatred and mutual resentment. If anyone happened to insult another by accident or hotheadedness, he hurried to make amends. Those, who did not want to forgive a brother who had sinned, were expelled from the monastery. The gait of the monks was modest. Upon meeting one another they bowed to each other. In church they stood at their designated place. Idle talk was not allowed, not only in the church, but everywhere else... Up to seven hundred brethren lived with Father Païssy then, and when they gathered in groups of a hundred, a hundred and fifty people for an obedience, then one of the brethren read a book or related some edifying tale. If anyone started an idle conversation, he was immediately stopped. In the cells one was writing books, another was plaiting... others were sewing klobuks and kamelaukions, knotting prayer ropes, manufacturing spoons and crosses, or engaged in various other handiwork. All were under the supervision of confessors and teachers. They went to them to confess their sins, and especially their thoughts, the origin of all evil deeds. And they did this twice a day. In the morning they reported what they had done in the night, and at night what they had done, said or thought in the day. All that was disclosed with humility, without shame and lies. Without a blessing no one dared even to eat some fruit, of which there was a lot in this country."

Of interest is also another narrative of Theophanes. When he returned from Moldavia, it so happened, that he was detained by the Turks. They asked who he was and from where he came. He showed them the entry document of Elder Païssy. Seeing the document, the Turks waved their arms and cried: "Oh, Païssy! Haydi, haydi!" i.e., "move on". Theophanes was surprised that even the Turks knew and honoured the blessed elder!

Theophanes also narrates the observance of orthodox purity in the community of Elder Païssy. When he was back in the Solovetsky Monastery, he instructed one of his disciples: "Beware of the followers of the schism. When I lived in Kiev, I did not see anybody who crossed himself with two fingers in the whole of Ukraine... In Moldavia, in the Neamts Monastery of Elder Païssy there were more than 700 brethren from different countries: Moldavians, Serbs, Bulgarians, Hungarians, Guzuls[35], Greeks, Armenians, Jews, Turks, Russians and Ukrainians. All of them crossed themselves with three fingers, and you didn't even hear about two fingers."

There is a story about a noble Greek, named Constantin Karadja who gave Elder Païssy a manuscript his father had of a hermit. The manuscript contained a sermon for monks. To express his gratitude, the ascetic sent the father a copy of the book in his own hand, in a beautiful, clear handwriting. The Greek wanted to go to the Monastery of the Ascension of the Lord, to bow to the icon of the Mother of God and to see the elder. He describes his journey with his wife from the city of Paşcani to the Neamts monastery and he tells his impressions meeting Elder Païssy. "For the first time in my life," says the Greek, "I saw with my own eyes unfeigned holiness personified. I was struck by his face, light and pale, without a droplet of blood, by his long white beard, shining like silver, and his extraordinary clean clothes... and the whole environment. His talk was gentle and completely sincere. He gave the impression of a man completely detached from the body."

Further, the Greek tells about the extraordinary hospitality of Elder Païssy. After quite a long conversation in the cell of the elder, the guests were taken to the room reserved for them, where they were also struck by the extraordinary cleanness. At the festive meal they and other honoured guests were served meat, poultry, fish, white bread, wine and sweets. And bread, fish and wine was generously given without any fee to all the pilgrims gathered in the courtyard of the monastery, and there were about three thousand of them.

Once again hard times set in. The brutal Russian-Turkish war of 1787-1791 began. The towns and villages of Moldavia emptied, the people were hiding in the mountains and forests, and anywhere where they could hide from the fury of the Turks. Elder Païssy provided shelter to local people in the Neamts Monastery as before in Dragomirna. The pantries of

the monastery were opened for them. Under the roof of the monastery women and children drew close together.
The Russian army entered Moldavia. The commander in chief Prince Potemkin and Ambrose, Archbishop of Poltava and Slovenia, arrived in the city of Iasi. The archbishop wanted to see the Neamts Monastery and Elder Païssy received him with respect. He spent two days in spiritual conversation with the elder. On Sunday Archbishop Ambrose celebrated the Divine Liturgy and elevated Païssy to the rank of archimandrite. Thus, Païssy, who was a native of Poltava, received the rank of archimandrite from Ambrose, the Archbishop of Poltava. This happened in 1790. At that time the Neamts Monastery became one of the most populated monastic communities of the Orthodox Church, uniting monks of more than ten nationalities.
In Neamts the elder most actively developed the work of translating and copying books. He drew in helpers and especially prepared them for this work. First of all, they were taught the Greek language. The most able were blessed by Elder Païssy to continue training at the Bucharest academy. The brethren worked on the books in their own cells or in a special room. Some worked with Elder Païssy in his cell. The manuscripts preserve the names of some of the most active helpers of the elder in this work. His closest aides were Hilarion, Macarius, and Honorius. In the manuscripts are mentioned hieroschemamonk Nicholas, hieromonk Ignatius, schemamonk Athanasius, confessor Nathaniel, priest Sophronius, priest Dositheus, monk Paul and scribe Michael, and the monks Joannicius, Sylvan, Nazarius, Mitrofan, Cyriacus, Gervasius, Philemon, Theophanes, Anthony, Sadof, hierodeacon Cornelius, deacon Timothy. Among the copyists of books were also lay people: Hyacinth, Gouri, Clement, Leontius, Haji Emanuel, Sophronius, Spiridon, Nicodemus, Gerasimus, Hierothey, Jerome, Sabbas, Sergius, Serapion, Plato and others.

Thanks to their hard work, a large number of corrected translations of patristic books and many copies appeared. According to a testimony of Professor A.I. Yatsimirskiy, who published an investigation on the topic in 1905, from the thousand manuscripts in the library of the Neamts Monastery written at different times in different languages, 276 date back to the time of Elder Païssy. More than 40 of them are copied by the elder. Moreover, according to the researcher, the manuscripts of the Neamts monastery are only part of the literary material, which was created by the elder and his companions. The manuscripts were spread over the monasteries, and they especially became diffused within Russia, including among the laity.

In 1787, Elder Païssy completed his most important literary work: a translation from the Greek language of the words of Saint Isaac the Syrian. He also worked on the works of saints Theodore the Studite, Barsanuphius, Gregory Palamas, Maximus the Confessor. The scholarship of one man may not be sufficient to properly understand and clearly describe patristic thought. For the translation of the holy Fathers personal experience of spiritual and ascetic life is necessary. The elder had spiritual experience and subtlety of understanding, enlightened by the constant practice of prayer, so he deeply penetrated into the meaning of the text. He knew how to pick the right words and precise words which revealed the contents. In so doing he chose words corresponding to the spirit of the original. His translations revealed the content, in spite of some clumsiness in constructions of speech.

The 24 translations by the ascetic of patristic texts, including texts of saints Anthony the Great, Gregory of Sinai, Peter of Damascus, and Simeon the New Theologian were compiled into a Philokalia collection.

In the Alexander Nevsky Lavra in Saint-Petersburg a circle of admirers and followers of Elder Païssy was formed, headed by the Metropolitan of Novgorod and Ladoga Gabriel. The elder sent the Philokalia with an accompanying letter to the metropolitan. With the blessing of the metropolitan the translation of the texts was examined by a group of teachers of the theological academy. The metropolitan encouraged them to consult some elders, who were experienced in the spiritual life, when checking the translation. He said that although those elders were unfamiliar with the subtleties of the Greek language, by their experience they had assimilated the contents of the patristic books and therefore they could give them useful indications. The book was published in 1793. This extensive anthology of religious texts has become a handbook not only for Russian monasticism, but also for many of the laity. Schemamonk Jerome, cenobite of the Anzersky monastery on one of the Solovetsky Islands, said that before the publication of the book, those "who wanted to learn the Jesus prayer went to Moldavia, to the Neamts monastery, to a real teacher... Elder Païssy. There they would receive instruction from him. Then they returned to Russia and lived by this instruction I have known such people," says the schemamonk. "But now, by the publication of the Philokalia, for those wishing to engage in prayer of the heart, an opportunity has opened up, because all the wiles of the devil are explained in this book." Elder Païssy worked as tirelessly as before: he directed the copying, laboured at translating patristic texts and he was in charge of the life of the community. But his strengths considerably lessened. According to the testimony of an eyewitness, the elder received the brethren and visitors in the last years of his life only from morning till noon. The rest of the time he spent alone in his cell. Then only the spiritual fathers of the monastery could come to him. According to an eyewitness, Elder Païssy took upon himself an amount of work exceeding natural human power. The grace of God strengthened him. He sat bent over on his bed. Nearby lay a variety of dictionaries, the Bible in Greek and Slavonic, a Greek and Slavonic grammar, as well as the book he was engaged in translating. Near the book stood lit candles. The elder sat hunched over like a little child. He wrote all night, forgetting about his bodily weakness and the need to rest. He used to be so absorbed in his activities that he did not hear the monastery bell, did not notice anything, did not answer questions. At such a time the servant did not let anyone in to him. When some urgent business appeared, he was forced to repeat the words many times to the elder, before receiving an answer. The elder was barely in a position to divert his attention away from the books, and if so only with pain and sighs. As he himself admitted: "For me, nothing is more excruciating than the trouble when I am translating to have to give an answer to some question. Then, before I manage to draw my mind back to the books, I get completely covered in perspiration."

Gradually the elder ceased translating himself, but until the last days of his life he reviewed and corrected manuscripts. According to the testimony of an eyewitness he felt especially weak after November 5, 1794. He spent four days in bed. On Sunday he felt better and he got up to go to the Liturgy. In the church he sat in his usual place. Then he went into the altar and partook of the holy Mysteries. After the service, the elder felt poorly and even supported by brethren he could hardly return to his cell. Three days passed. The brothers Honorius and Martyrios did not allow anybody to see him, except for those closest to him, as the elder wanted to stay in complete silence. On the fourth day, feeling death approaching, Elder Païssy partook of the holy Mysteries once more. Then he called two senior spiritual fathers, Sophronius and Sylvester, and gave them a blessing to pass on to the whole community. Elder Païssy did not appoint a successor, leaving that to the will of God, the election by the Mother of God and the wish

of the brethren. He quietly departed to the Lord, as if falling asleep, on November 15, 1794, at the age of 72 years.
For the burial of the father superior a multitude of people gathered together in Neamts: monks and laymen, priests, nobles and common people. The funeral service of the elder in the church of the Ascension of the Lord was performed with the whole monastery. He was buried on the right side of the entrance of the church. The day after the burial Benjamin, the bishop of Tuma, came to celebrate a Liturgy and a memorial service. Soon, the Bishop appointed spiritual father Sophronius to be the father superior of the monastery with the consent of the brethren and the blessing of Metropolitan Jacob. At the grave of Elder Païssy a plate was placed with an inscription in Moldavian and Slavonic: "Here rests our blessed Father Hieroschemamonk and Archimandrite Elder Païssy, Ukranian, who came from Mount Athos with 60 disciples to Moldavia, and gathered a multitude of brethren,, renewed the coenobium, and departed to the Lord on November 15, 1794, in the days of the pious ruler Michael Suţu the commander and his Eminence Metropolitan Jacob." One of the disciples, hieroschemamonk John Diakovskiy, composed in the poetic form: "Graveside weeping for Elder Païssy from all his spiritual children."
The brethren of the Neamts monastery had undoubting confidence in the power of prayer of Elder Païssy and esteemed him as a great servant of God. Shortly after his death, a service (stichera and a canon) was composed in honour of "our blessed Father and Elder, hieroschemamonk and Archimandrite Païssy."
When Elder Païssy was still alive he had an extraordinary gift of fiery, sorrowful prayer, during which his light and magnificent face always shone with an inner fire. His servant elder, schemamonk Mitrofan, once came to the cell of the elder in Dragomirna. He said a prayer, bowed and said, "Bless me, fa-

ther." The elder did not answer. "I looked at him," recounts the servant, "and I saw that his face was as on fire, while it usually was white and pale. I was terrified. After standing there for a while, I repeated the prayer in a louder voice. Again the elder didn't answer. I realized that he was absorbed in prayer... After standing there a little more, I went out without telling anyone what I had seen." In the course of time, the same monk saw the face of the elder full of light twice, while he elder was in conversation with the brethren.

The servant of God had the ability to foresee events. He predicted the death of Governor Grigore Ghica: more than once he saw in a dream a sword hanging on a thread above the head of the governor.

There was one brother who saddened the elder. Païssy reminded him often to correct his life, but the brother did not listen. Three days after a particularly tearful admonition of the elder, the brother drowned. Another brother wanted to go away. The elder implored him not to go outside of the monastery and, finally, he said to him in tears: "Listen to me, because you will not reach the place where you want to go!" The brother did not listen, and four days later he died on the way.

There were cases of miraculous cures through the prayers of Elder Païssy, which he in his deep humility entirely attributed to the intercession of the Mother of God.

Among the ascetic's endowments of grace was the gift of deep self-knowledge, about which the teacher of silence, venerable Isaac the Syrian, whom the elder loved so much, said: "He, who can see himself, is more blessed than he who has seen an angel."

After venerable Sergius, venerable Païssy revived in Russia the school of eldership, which throughout the XIXth century and later brought fertile fruits to the Glinsk and Optina deserts and other monasteries of the Russian church.

In general, according to a study by Archpriest Sergius Chetverikov, the spiritual movement in Russia under the influence of Elder Païssy can be divided into three main currents: the northern, central and southern movement. "The northern movement had as its main centres: the Solovetsky Monastery, Valaam, the Alexander Nevsky Monastery, and the Alexander-Svirsky Monastery. The central movement was established mainly in Moscow, in the Vladimir province, in the Optina Monastery in the Kaluga province, in the Bryansk Monastery in the Orlov province, in the Roslavl forests of the Smolensk eparchy, and in the Beloberezhsky Monastery. The southern movement was centred in the Ploschansky Monastery of the Orlov eparchy, the Glinsk Monastery of the Kursk eparchy, and other places. These monasteries should be considered only as the most prominent or starting points of Païssy's school, which actually covers not only tens but hundreds of Russian monasteries."

The spiritual gift of venerable Païssy Velichkovsky fully ripened, leaving a legacy of abundant fruit. His students and subsequent generations saw the main merit of the elder in having renewed the monastic life. Thanks to his efforts to correct and translate patristic texts the study of the works of the holy fathers revived.

How did it happen that he took this mission upon himself? He had not aspired to it. Moreover, he accepted it as if against his own wish. Elder Païssy saw himself as a man whose personal plans were thwarted by God's providence during his whole life. Therefore he did not consider the work that was entrusted to him as his own, but as a work of the Spirit of God.

He acquired the gift of prayer of the heart, and was the teacher of "inner prayer". The elder had the gift to spiritually guide a great number of brethren. More than a thousand monks were in his care. He had the rare ability to unite brethren of different nationalities.

From his youth, Païssy had cherished the desire to leave the world and enter a monastery. "In a period when monastic life was so relaxed and showed only its outer aspect, Païssy revealed that there exists a real monasticism, there really is the mystery of obedience, which brings great benefit to beginners, leading them forward on the path of spiritual understanding, that there really is active life combined with contemplation or prayer of the heart, the kind that is brought down out of the mind into the heart," wrote his servant schemamonk Mitrofan.

Païssy had tried to find a spiritual teacher with whom to live in obedience, and confessed that *he* had not been able to find one just like that. "My inner disposition from my youth made me more inclined to commit myself to obedience, but I was deemed unworthy - that is how I am damned - to be vouchsafed this divine gift."

If he had found what he wanted, perhaps we would never have known Elder Païssy.

He had firmly promised himself that he would never live in large monasteries, where there is comfort and honour, but as a result he settled in the largest and most famous orthodox monastery of the time.

The ascetic did not aspire to become a priest; he hid on Athos to escape that dignity. But only a few years later, he was forced to accept the ordination, yielding to the persistence of the brethren who had gathered around him.

His life was continuously remodelling itself; he had to discard his solemnly taken definitive decisions, because of the course of events, in which he could later recognize God's will.

Païssy, by his own testimony, did not find a spiritual father and therefore he began to use the Holy Scripture and works of the holy fathers as a spiritual guide.

Schemamonk Mitrofan wrote: "He was taught by God and also by the teachings of the holy Fathers, while studying and translating their works. The ancient holy Fathers always kept their eyes on those, who served as an example for them, who were shining with the light of a God-pleasing life and with the truth of their learning. There were also teachers, from whom they could learn by living with them. They stayed with them from their youth, contemplating their blameless life and teachings. Those teachers were like living pillars [of faith]. So the students also became living pillars and light when *they* became teachers of the monastic life... Our blessed father, in contrast, did not have a similar teacher... He worked diligently, enlightened by God's grace, humbly sought and gained in his own heart the source of water, which gave him and others abundantly to drink. And the fuller the buckets he drew out of there, the more abundantly flowed the source."

Of the three types of monastic life, life in solitary seclusion, life at two and life in a community, Païssy chose the last. But that was not the life that he had dreamed about. He abandoned his homeland for a life in solitude and poverty, living with only one brother, in obedience to an experienced spiritual father.

As far back as Athos first Bessarion had come to him. Païssy considered Bessarion not a disciple, but a brother. After that new brethren joined. A small community of 12 monks is formed. Although he was compelled to do so, Païssy made a kind of natural transition from the middle path to the coenobitic path. But exactly this transition allowed him to use the special gifts of the middle path in the community life. On the middle path "instead of a teacher one has the teachings of our holy fathers, and instead of a father one obeys each other in the love of God". The ascetic does not reconstruct and reform monasticism. He revives it and makes it apt to draw from the source of grace.

In 1789 he wrote the aged nun Nazariya, whom he had urged to leave her seclusion in the mountains and to create a community in Văratec. *"I beg you, drive out all aversion and all grief from your soul and with all zeal and joy fulfil the service which the Lord entrusted to you, knowing that all the temptations and sorrows of this age are transient and temporary, while the reward and joy that occur through them are eternal and timeless. No doubt, the many troubles and all the blame that you have to endure now, seem to you to harm you and to diminish your virtue, contrary to the quiet that you enjoyed in the mountains. But while amongst the sisters, serving them for the sake of their salvation, do not think at all that this harms you, on the contrary, it will bring you a great and glorious reward and a crown even more resplendent. As love truly is the greatest of all the virtues, so is the work, which is entrusted to you, greater than anything else, because it is a work of love."*

Venerable Paissy's Doctrine of mental or inner Prayer (An arrangement by Guram Kochi and Irina Veris)

"As I am dust and ashes, I mentally fall on the knees of my heart before the unapproachable majesty of Thy divine glory, and I pray Thee, my most sweet Jesus, only begotten Son and Word of God, the radiance of the glory and the image of the hypostasis of the Father! Enlighten my darkened mind and thoughts, and grant Your grace to my accursed soul, so that this work of mine will serve to the glory of Thy most holy name and to the benefit of those, who want to mentally cling to Thee, our God, through the sacred inner work of mental prayer, and who want to carry Thee, priceless bead, incessantly in their soul and in their heart!"
Blessed Elder, Schemamonk and Archimandrite Paissy Velichkovsky

In ancient times, the most holy exercise of *mental prayer* [prayer performed in the mind] was shining in many places, wherever the *holy fathers* [Christian ascetics] stayed. Therefore there were many teachers of this spiritual inner work. For this reason, our holy fathers, when talking about it, showed only its ineffable spiritual benefit, I think, having no need to write about the experience of doing this [technique,], which would be suitable for beginners. So when they *did* write a little about it, then for those who have the experience of mental [inner] work it is clear, but for the unfamiliar it is not clear at all. Some of them saw that there are very few true and *undeluded* teachers of this inner work and feared that the true doctrine of the beginning of this mental prayer would be lost. So they described the very beginning and the experience of how to train beginners to enter with the mind [attention] *the lands of the heart* [the inner, spiritual space of the heart], and truly pray there with the mind *without delusions.* It is the divine teaching of these fathers on this subject which it is necessary to elaborate here.

Saint Symeon the New Theologian says the following about the beginning of this inner work: "The core of the true and undeluded contemplation and prayer is that during the prayer the mind guards the heart and stays constantly inside the heart [focused in the heart] and sends up prayers to God from the depths of the heart. When the mind thus is being focused in the heart will taste, that the Lord is good (Ps. 34:8), and is delighted, then it will not be willing to ever leave the [inner, spiritual] room of the heart. And together with the apostle it will say: "It is good for us to be here" (Mt. 17:4). And incessantly examining the room of the heart, the mind will invent a certain way to drive away all the thoughts of the enemy that keep coming there." And even more clearly he says about this: "As soon as the mind finds the [inner, spiritual] room of the heart, immediately it sees something it has never seen: it sees in the middle of the heart the air and the whole of itself full of light and understanding. And from that point onward, no matter from where a thought may have appeared, before it will go into the heart and develop, the mind will immediately drive it away and destroy it by the invocation of Jesus Christ. Hence the mind, which feels hate towards demons, brings forth its natural anger against them and banishes and conquers [them], its mental enemies. And other things you will learn with the help of God through thorough guarding of the mind, [by] keeping Jesus in the heart" (A word on three kinds of prayer).

Venerable Nicephorus the Faster, who taught even more clearly about the mind entering the heart, says: "First of all, let your life be silent, without any worldly, everyday worries and at peace [without enmity]. Then, go into your room, shut the door, and sit down in some corner and do as I tell you.

You know that the breath we breathe is air. We exhale it essentially with the heart. The heart is the cause of the life and warmth of the body. The heart uses air to let out warmth and give itself coolness by breathing. The *reason* for this action, or I should say the *instrument*, is the lungs, which the Creator created as inflatable, as some kind of pump, that can conveniently input and output the surroundings, i.e., the air. Thus, the heart, by means of the breath drawing in cold and giving off heat, constantly performs the action for which it is made: to support life. While you, having sat down and focusing your mind at the same time forcing your attention to enter the heart along with the inhaled air. And when it has entered there, then that what is yet to come will already be not mirthless and not joyless. Therefore, brother, train the mind not to go out of there too soon, because at first the mind gets cast down by the inner seclusion and tightness. But when it gets used to it, it already does not want to wander off, because the kingdom of heaven is within us. When we think of the kingdom of heaven [being focused with our mind] in our heart and try to find it by means of pure prayer, then all external affairs will seem vile and hateful.

If you immediately, as I said, enter with your mind the room of the heart that I showed you, then give thanks to God and glorify Him, and rejoice, and keep doing this inner work all the time, and it will teach you what you do not know. You should know too, that the mind, when it is there, should not be silent or be idle, but it should be continuously engaged in repeating and studying these words: "Lord Jesus Christ, Son of God, have mercy on me!" And this prayer should never stop. It prevents the mind from becoming arrogant and makes it] elusive and inaccessible to calumnies and attacks from the enemy and elevates it daily to love and longing for the Divine.

If you have worked a lot on this, brother, and still cannot enter into the lands of the heart [the inner, spiritual room of the heart], as we have instructed you, just do what I tell you, and with God's help you will find what you are seeking. It is known to you, that the reason of each person is situated in the chest. When our lips are silent it is there, inside the chest, that we talk and reason, and say prayers and psalms, and other things. Take away from this reason every [other] thought (you are able to, if you only want), and let it say: "Lord Jesus Christ, Son of God, have mercy on me", and work to invoke this inside, instead of all sorts of other thoughts. When you hold out like this for some time, then an entrance into your heart will no doubt open itself for you, as we have written to you, and as we ourselves have learned from experience. And with this sought-after, sweet attention the whole choir of the virtues will come to you [i.e., in your soul all other divine qualities will also appear]: love, joy, peace, and others."

Divine Gregory of Sinai teaches how to perform with the mind in the heart the salvational invocation of the Lord. He said: "Sit down in the morning on a narrow chair or bench, and let the mind go down from the head to the heart, and keep it there [i.e., concentrate your mind, your attention, in the heart]. Bow your head with strain and feeling a lot of pain in the chest, shoulders and neck; constantly call with your mind or soul: "Lord Jesus Christ, have mercy on me!" If, perhaps, because of tightness and pain, and the frequent invocation of the prayer, the prayer causes you distress, then move the mind to another part of the prayer and say: "Son of God, have mercy on me!" You should not often alternate the two parts, because trees that are often transplanted don't take root. Constrain the breathing of your lungs so that you do not breathe boldly [i.e., breathe easily, almost imperceptibly]; for the movement of air that comes from the heart stirs up thoughts and darkens the mind and brings it back from there, makes it a prisoner of oblivion or compels it to practice instead of one thing something else and it [the mind] becomes insensitive to that to which it should not show insensitivity. If you see the uncleanliness of evil spirits, i.e., thoughts that occur or appear in your mind, do not be horrified, but also if good reflections about some things appear to you, do not heed them. Hold your breath as long as possible, while containing the mind in the heart, and constantly and frequently call the Lord Jesus. Then you will quickly crush and destroy them, wounding them invisibly with the divine name as John of the Ladder says: "Hit warriors [demons] with the name of Jesus, because there is no stronger weapon, neither in heaven, nor on earth."

And again Gregory of Sinai, teaching about silence and prayer, and how to sit when doing it [such inner work]: "Sometimes it is better to sit on a small chair, making it less comfortable for you, bend sometimes on your bed for a while, to have a little rest. You should be patient while sitting for it is said: "Persevere in prayer" (Col. 4:2), and you ought not to get up too soon from prayer; don't give in to the lack of spirit because of difficulties due to the infirmity of the body and the mental invocation and the constant straining of the mind. The prophet Jeremiah also prophesized thus: "I am black; astonishment hath taken hold on me." (Jr. 8:21). So, bow your head and focus the mind in the heart, if your heart has opened itself to you, call on for help the Lord Jesus. Thus suffering pain in the shoulders and head, endure it with strength and zeal, trying to find the Lord in the heart: "The kingdom of heaven suffers violence, and the violent take it by force." (Mt. 11:12) et al. And he also talks about how to say the prayer: "The fathers explained it like this: Some say "Lord Jesus Christ, Son of God, have mercy on me!", i.e. the whole prayer, others say only a part "Jesus, Son of God, have mercy on me" and that is more convenient for those whose mind is infirm and who are in their [spiritual] infancy. No one can by himself, without the Spirit, call the name of the Lord Jesus in a pure and perfect way "but by the Holy Ghost." (1 Cor. 12:3). But being as if an infant, who cannot talk, he is not able to yet. He should not out of laziness often change the words he says, but rarely, so as to keep his attention. Again: some teach to say the prayer with the lips, others mentally, and I allow the one and the other. Sometimes the mind gets exhausted and bored with saying the prayer, sometimes the mouth. Therefore we must pray both with the mouth and the mind, but it is better to call out silently and undisturbed by the voice. The voice should not disturb the feelings and the attention of the mind. It should not get in the way as long as the mind is still adapting and has not reached its goal, has not received from the Spirit the power to pray firmly and perfectly. Then there will no longer be the need to say the words with the mouth, and the person will even not be able to, because he will be able to do the inner work of prayer with the mind alone."

Thus, the aforementioned holy fathers, as shown, present a very clear teaching and their experience of teaching mental inner work to beginners. Now that we have assimilated this lesson, we can get acquainted with the teachings of other saints about mental prayer, teachings that are expressed more covertly.

As this Divine prayer is greater than any other monastic work and is, according to the teaching of the holy fathers, the pinnacle of all improvements, the source of virtues, a most subtle work of the mind carried out invisibly in the depth of the heart, so are the most subtle, invisible nets of manifold delusions and reveries, barely comprehensible to the human mind, that the invisible enemy of our salvation stretches out around the prayer. Therefore, he who strives to learn this Divine inner work, should, in the opinion of Saint Symeon the New Theologian, give himself body and soul, to obedience, in line with the Holy Scriptures. I.e., he has to give himself over to the full curtailment of his will and reasoning by a man who fears God, a zealous guardian of His divine commandments, who has experience with this mental work; who is able, according to the writings of the holy fathers, to show him who lives in obedience [disciple, novice] the correct way to salvation, the way of the inner work of mental prayer, secretly done by the mind being [focused] in the heart. True obedience of the mind is indispensable to ensure he might be freed from all worries, concerns and passions of this world and of the body. After all, how can someone not be free if he entrusts the care of his soul and his body to God and, in God, to his spiritual father? He will be able to avoid all delusions and nets of the devil by humility, which is born from obedience, according to the testimony of Saint John of the Ladder and many other holy fathers, and then he may quietly and silently, without any harm, constantly practice this mental work with great benefit for his soul.

If someone having given himself into obedience did not find in his spiritual father an experienced and skilful teacher of this Divine mental prayer, then he should not give way to despair. Nowadays is a grievous and piteous time, because the number of experienced teachers of this inner work continues to diminish. But being in true obedience according to the commandments of God (and not arbitrarily[36] and, in particular not wilfully[37], without obedience, which is usually followed by delusion), and having put all his hope in both God and his spiritual father, let him obey in faith and love, instead of a real teacher, the teachings of our venerable fathers, who, inspired by Divine grace, have expounded in the smallest details the practice of this Divine inner work and adopt from them instructions about this prayer. In any case, the Grace of God, through the prayers of the holy fathers, will help him and make him understand beyond doubt how to learn this divine work.

The divine work of sacred mental prayer was the unceasing occupation of our ancient God-bearing fathers. In many places in the desert and in cenobite monasteries this work began to shine like a sun: on mount Sinai, in the Egyptian hermitages in the Nitrian desert, in Jerusalem and in monasteries located in the vicinity of Jerusalem, in a word, all over the Middle East, but also in Constantinople, on Mount Athos and on islands of the Mediterranean. And in recent times, by the grace of Christ, also in Russia. By this mental attention to sacred prayer many of our God-bearing fathers started burning like seraphim, with a flame of love for God and through God for their neighbour. They became strict keepers of the commandments of God. They cleansed their souls and hearts of all the vices of their old self, and were awarded to be chosen vessels of the Holy Spirit. They were filled with His manifold Divine gifts; they were in their lifetime luminaries and pillars of fire for the universe. They performed countless miracles and in deed and word they led many human souls to salvation. Many of them having received secretly God's inspiration wrote books with their teachings about Divine mental prayer. Those books, full of wisdom of the Holy Spirit, are equal in strength to the Holy Scriptures of the Old and New Testaments. And this was arranged by the particular Providence of God, so that in the last times this divine work would not be forgotten. Because of our sins, God allowed many of these books to be destroyed by the Saracens when they conquered the Byzantine Empire. And thanks to God's care some have survived to our times.

The orthodox have always treated mental prayer and maintaining the paradise of the heart [prayer of the heart] with the utmost reverence, as something [practice] full of spiritual benefit., It is exactly through the work of the mental prayer that the monks, choosing the right path, dwell at Jesus' feet with a love that cannot be taken away from them .[38] Thus they succeed in achieving perfection in fulfilling His divine commandments, and they become a light and illumination for the world. Gregory Palamas, archbishop of Thessalonica, the most lucent among our fathers, living in perfect obedience and incessantly doing the holy work of mental prayer, shone on the holy Mount Athos like a sun by the gifts of the Holy Spirit.

About mental prayer it says in the New Testament: "Pray without ceasing." (1 Thess. 5:17), "I will pray with the spirit, and I will pray with the understanding also (1 Cor. 14:15)," "singing with grace in your hearts to the Lord (Col. 3:16)," "God hath sent forth the Spirit of his Son into your hearts, crying, Abba, Father (Gal. 4:6), "rather speak five words with understanding, than ten thousand words in an unknown tongue (1 Cor. 14:19)." As the Lord Himself says in the Gospel, "that your fruit should remain: that whatsoever ye shall ask of the Father in my name, he may give it you (Jn. 15:16)." and also: "In my name shall they cast out devils (Mk. 16:17)." Because His name is eternal life: "But these are written, that ye might believe that Jesus is the Christ, the Son of God; and that believing ye might have life through His name (Jn. 20:31)." And you profess the Holy Spirit by invoking Christ: "No man speaking by the Spirit of God calleth Jesus accursed: and no man can say that Jesus is the Lord, but by the Holy Ghost (1 Cor. 12:3)." Invoking the name of our Lord Jesus Christ is salvational for us. Is the human mind with which the prayer is said damned? Impossible, because we know, that God created man in His own image and likeness. So the soul of man was pure and without blemish when it was created by God. That also means that the mind, which is the first sense of the soul, as sight is the first sense of the body, was without blemish. Can we condemn the heart, in which, as on an altar, the mind solemnly brings the secret sacrifice of prayer to God? No. Being God's creation, the heart, as well as the entire human body, is beautiful. If the invocation of the name of Jesus is salvational, and the mind and heart of man are the work of God, then why not send up our prayers to the Most Sweet Jesus from the depth of the heart with the mind and ask Him for mercy? Do not think that God does not hear the prayers that are said secretly in the heart, and hears only those which are pronounced by the lips. God is a knower of hearts and He knows exactly all the most subtle thoughts of the heart, and even future ones, and He knows everything as omniscient God. He Himself demands precisely such a secret prayer, as a pure and undefiled sacrifice, being sent up from the depths of the heart, when He gave the commandment: "But thou, when thou prayest, enter into thy closet, and when thou hast shut thy door, pray to thy Father which is in secret; and thy Father which seeth in secret shall reward thee openly (Mt. 6:6)."

The ecumenical teacher Saint John Chrysostom, in Conversation0 Nineteen on the Gospel of Matthew, sees God-given wisdom of the Holy Spirit not in that prayer, which is said only by the lips and the tongue, but in the most secret, speechless prayer, which is sent from the depth of the heart. He teaches us to pray not with physical movements and not with a loud voice, but with a most zealous effort of the will, in silence, with contrition of thoughts and inner tears, with remorse, and with one's mental doors closed [to distractions]. He cites the God-seer Moses, Saint Anne and righteous Abel from the divine Scriptures to testify about this prayer, when he says: "But is your heart bleeding? [Then] you won't be able to withhold your cry, because to pray and to beseech the way I told you is appropriate to someone who is suffering greatly. Also Moses suffered, and prayed like this, and his anguish was heard, and that is why God said to him: "Wherefore criest thou unto Me? (Ex. 14:15)." Saint Anne also, she accomplished all she wanted, but it was not her voice that was heard, it was because her heart wept. And Abel, did he not pray in silence, even when his life had come to an end? Even his blood gave off a voice that sounded louder than the voice of a trumpet. You also, weep like holy Moses, I will not forbid you. Rend your heart, as the prophet commanded, and not your clothes. From the depths call upon God: "Out of the depths have I cried unto thee, O Lord (Ps. 129:1)", the prophet says. From below, from the heart, stir up your voice. Make your prayer your sacrament. After all, you do not pray to people, but to God the Omnipresent, Who has heard you before your voice has reached Him and Who knows your unspoken thoughts. If you pray like this, you will receive a great reward. Since He is invisible, he wants your prayer also to be invisible." You see, friends, that according to the invincible pillars of orthodoxy there is another prayer apart from the one uttered with the mouth. A secret, invisible, silent prayer from the depth of the heart raised to God. As a pure offering it is accepted by the Lord as the perfume of spiritual fragrance. God is pleased with it when he sees that the mind which primarily must be devoted to Him, united with Him in prayer.

Maybe you happened to see or hear about someone who practised this prayer and went crazy, or took some delusion for the truth, or harmed his soul, so you thought that mental prayer could cause such harm? In fact it is not at all like that. Sacred mental prayer, as the God-bearing fathers testify, being performed with the grace of God, cleanses from all human passions, inspires to diligently keep the commandments of God and keeps one unharmed from all the enemy's arrows and delusions. But if someone bold practises this prayer wilfully, not guided by the teachings of the holy fathers, without the help and advice of an experienced father, and if he is arrogant, full of passions and weak, if he lives without obedience and submission and also if he seeks to live the life of a recluse without being worthy of it because of his wilfulness, such a person, indeed, I would state, will easily fall in all the nets and delusions of the devil. What now? Is this prayer the reason for these delusions? No. If mental prayer is considered harmful, then a knife is harmful too, because it so happens that a small child when playing with it will cut himself because he is foolish. Then you also need to forbid soldiers the use of swords, which they raise against the enemy, if one reckless soldier stabbed himself with his sword. A knife and a sword are not the cause of any vice, but only expose the recklessness of those who cut or stab themselves. And in this way the spiritual sword of *sacred* mental prayer is not the cause of any vice. Only wilful arbitrariness and pride of the wilful are the cause of devilish delusions and all kinds of psychological harm.

The patristic books are the most suitable reading for monastics. They contain all the wisdom of life according to the Gospel. For monks, they are also indispensable for psychological use and correction, and to acquire a true, healthy, undeluded and humble mind. For these reasons patristic books are as indispensable [for the monks as breath for the life of the body. God would never allow you to lapse into temptation if you thus read patristic books. Moreover, through this inner work He would have ignite you with His Divine grace in His unspeakable love, so that you would have been inspired to say with the apostle: "Who shall separate us from the love of Christ (Rom. 8:35)?" This love you would have been favoured to achieve by the exercise of this mental prayer. And you would not only not condemn it, but you would try to give your life for it, because you would sense in deeds and by experience the ineffable benefit to your soul of this mental attention [prayer]. As you do not read the books of our venerable fathers with unquestioning faith or read them but do not trust them or just ignore them, you fall into ungodly reasoning.

And to help you and all doubters to get rid of such harm for the soul, I will find no other appropriate remedy than to endeavour, as far as God by His grace will assist and help me, to show that our God-bearing fathers, enlightened by the grace of God, consolidate the edifice of their soul-nurturing teaching - about this most holy prayer that is secretly performed by the mind in the heart - on the unshakable rock of Holy Scripture. The grace of God will secretly touch your souls to help you see plainly and clearly the truth of the teachings of the holy fathers. When you have thus been healed of this psychological illness of ungodly reasoning, repent most sincerely to God about your vacillation and you will be favoured with His mercy and His perfect forgiveness for your delusion.

Before indicating from where this divine prayer originates, the following should be taken into consideration: we know from the writings of our God-bearing fathers, that there are two kinds of mental prayer. One is [the prayer] of beginners, referring to the action, and the other is [the prayer] of the perfect, which appertains to vision [contemplation]. The first is the beginning, and the second is the end, because the action is the ascent to the vision. You should know that, in the words of saint Gregory of Sinai, there are eight first visions. He enumerates them as follows: "We say that there are eight primary visions. The first - the vision of God invisible, without beginning and uncreated, the cause of all that exists, the one Trinity, which has always existed before the whole of creation. The second - a vision of the ranks and characteristics of the intelligent [bodiless] powers.[39] The third - the vision of the qualities of material beings. Fourth - the vision of the providential descent of the Word [the incarnation of Christ]. Fifth – the vision of the universal resurrection. Sixth - the vision of the second and awesome coming of Christ. Seventh - the vision of eternal torment. Eighth - the kingdom of heaven, which has no end." Having presented this knowledge I can

now impart within the limitations of my feeble mind in what sense action and vision must be understood.
It should be known (and I address myself to people in general, like myself), that the entire monastic achievement consists in forcing oneself, with God's help:
to love God and one's neighbour; to be meek, humble and patient, and to observe all the other commandments of God and the holy fathers;
to be perfectly obedient to God in body and soul, to observe the fast and vigil, to be in tears, to make bows and to do all other practices to macerate the body;
to most zealously carry out the church and the cell rule;
to do the silent inner work of mental prayer;
to lament and remember death,
and in which the mind still controls the human will and desire, can reliably be called action [work], but in no way vision [contemplation]. But, in some of the writings of the holy fathers such mental prayer is also called "vision", because the mind, like the eye of the soul, can [figuratively] be called vision.
First a person has to purify his soul and heart from all the filth of the passions of the soul and the body. He can do this with God's help and by the aforementioned inward work, but more so by profound humility. After that, God's grace will take the mind as a little child by the hand. Divine Grace is like a mother we all have in common. It leads the mind which It has first cleansed in stages to the spiritual visions [described by Gregory of Sinai], and reveals to it, proportional to its measure of purification, the unspeakable and incomprehensible divine Mysteries. And this really is what is called true spiritual vision. And that is the same as visionary [contemplative] prayer, or in the words of Saint Isaac, pure prayer, which causes awe and vision. But nobody can enter these visions by his own will, by arbitrary inward work [spiritual prac-

tices], unless God visits him and by His Grace leads him into these visions. But if someone boldly tries to ascend to such visions without the light of grace, then he should know that he does not have visions, but that he imagines dreams, that he dreams and imagines with the spirit of dreams, according to Saint Gregory of Sinai (Ch. 130). Such is the discourse on active and visionary [contemplative] prayer. But now the moment has come to explain from where divine mental prayer originates:

Let it be known that, according to the reliable testimony of our God-wise, venerable and God-bearing Father Nilus the faster of Sinai, mental divine prayer was given by God Himself to primordial man already in heaven as a work befitting the perfect. Saint Nilus instructed those who pray [ascetics, zealots] to protect the fruit of their prayer zealously and courageously so that their labour would not be vain. He says: "Having prayed as it is proper, anticipate the unexpected, and stand with courage, guarding your fruit. After all you are appointed to this from the beginning: "cultivate and tend" (Gen. 2:15). Therefore, having produced, do not leave the work without guard for otherwise you will not receive any benefit from prayer (Ch. 49)."

These words were explained by venerable Nilus, hermit of Sora. In Russia Nilus of Sora shone as a sun, owing to his labour of mental prayer, as is evident from his God-wise book. He says: "This saint quoted words from ancient times: "cultivate and tend", because the Scripture says that, after God had created Adam, He placed him in paradise to cultivate and tend it. Here Saint Nilus of Sinai explains that the work in paradise [cultivating] is [in fact] prayer, and tending - the guarding [of one's heart and mind] against evil thoughts after praying." Likewise, also venerable Dorotheus says primordial man, who was placed by God in paradise, lived in prayer. This he writes in his first sermon. These testimonies show that when God created man in His image and likeness, He led him into the paradise of delight to cultivate the immortal gardens, i.e., Divine thoughts, most pure, most elevated and most perfect, according to Saint Gregory the Theologian. And this [cultivation] is nothing else but that he, pure of heart and soul, should abide in visionary, sacredly performed by mental blessed prayer, i.e. in the most delightful vision of God, and would courageously guard it as the apple of his eye, as a work of paradise, so that it would never subside in his heart and soul. Therefore, the glory of the sacred and divine mental prayer is great. Its limits, i.e., its beginning and its perfection were given to man by God in paradise, from where it [therefore] originates.

But it [this mental inner prayer] became far more glorious when the most holy Virgin, the Theotokos, more honourable than the Cherubim and more glorious beyond compare than the Seraphim, being in the Holy of Holies, ascended in mental prayer to the utmost height of the vision of God. She was vouchsafed to become the spacious abode for Him, Whom all creation cannot contain, God's Word, Who hypostatically accommodated Himself in Her, and Who, [being conceived] without semen, was born from Her, for the salvation of mankind. Thus testifies the irrefutable pillar of orthodoxy, who is numbered among the saints, our father Gregory Palamas, archbishop of Thessaloniki in "Sermon on the Presentation in the Temple of our most holy Mistress Theotokos and Ever Virgin Mary." He says that the blessed Virgin Mother of God being in the Holy of Holies, and having truly learned from the Holy Scriptures, which were read in the temple every Saturday, of the perdition of the human race as a result of its disobedience. She felt strong compassion and received from God mental prayer for the rapid forgiveness and salvation of the human race. I present here also a few words of Saint Gregory, words that are worthy of an angelic intelligence: "This divine

Virgin was filled with pity for the entire human race and wondered how to find healing and treatment equal in strength to such suffering. Shortly after, She found a way to address herself with the whole mind to God, and learned this prayer for us in order to call upon [God the Trinity], to attract Him quickly to us so that He Himself should forgive us, extinguish the fire, which ruins the opulence of the soul, and to re-unite His creation [man] to Himself, having thus healed the feeble. Thus, the blessed Virgin preferred the mental prayer as the most wondrous and glorious [means], which is better than any word. She investigated what is the most comely/ and appropriate way to talk to God, and He Himself initiated Her to come to Him, or rather, She was the God-chosen Virgin of Prayer... The Virgin saw that nothing that exists is better than that [mental prayer] for man. She applies zealous efforts to prayer, creates a new, larger and more perfect [path of ascent to God], and invents, and acts, and after that presents action as the most elevated ascent to vision, because vision is as much more than action, as truth is higher than dreams.

Therefore, someone who wants to taste the blessings of the coming age should covet to imitate the First and the One to the utmost of his capabilities the Ever Virgin Bride of God, who has renounced from infancy the external, earthly world for the sake of the inner [world] ... In search of the prayer zealots most need to reach Communion with God, the Virgin found sacred silence, i.e., the silence of the mind: remoteness from the world, forgetting what is earthly and keeping the secrets of the heavens.

So action, as the true ascent to the vision of God, is like a brief manual for the soul of someone who really has accomplished it [action]. All other virtues [other than the vision of God] are as the treatment of mental illnesses and evil passions as a result of depression that has taken root. But the vision of God is the fruit of a soul that is healthy and well, like a kind of final perfection and image of God's works. A person becomes likened to God not by words or sensible moderation with regard to the visible world. Those are all earthly, base, human things. But we do become like God by abiding in silence[40], because with that we turn away and move away from the earth and ascend to God. Spending days and nights in prayer and supplication in the room of silent existence, we somehow approach that Unapproachable and Blissful Essence. Those who live in such a way, who purify the heart with sacred silence and merge inconceivably with Him Who is holy beyond the senses and the mind, will see God in themselves, as in a mirror. Thus, silence is a rather swift and abbreviated guide, the most successful guide, which unites with God, especially those who observe it [silence] in its plenitude. But the Virgin, Who abided in silence from Her childhood, how about Her? She kept silent from her very childhood and of all women it was She Who gave birth to God-Man, the Word, alone, without having known a man... Therefore She is immaculate. She renounced the very, so to speak, everyday existence and agitation. She moved away from people and avoided a sinful way of life. She chose a hidden and unsocial life and stayed inaccessible. Here She was free from all physical relationships, here She could escape all contacts and attachment to everything and She surpassed the indulgence of the body itself. She focused Her whole mind to abide with Him in communication, attention, and in an unceasing Divine prayer. And through it [prayer], in Herself, above diverse agitations and thoughts, and absolutely above all forms and objects, She found a new and indescribable path to heaven, which is, so to say, to mentally keep silent. And being zealously attentive with her mind to silence she excels all creation and creatures. Far better than Moses She sees the glory of God, and contemplates the Divine Grace. It is not in the least subject to the power of the senses. Undefiled souls and minds rejoice in the good of this sacred

vision. When She partook of it [the vision of God], She - using the words of the divine hymnographers – manifests Herself as a light cloud of true water of life, and as Dawn for the mind and as fiery Chariot of the Word" (Saint Gregory Palamas).
From these words of divine Gregory Palamas an intelligent person can clearly understand that the immaculate Virgin Theotokos, when She was abiding in the Holy of Holies, ascended to the utmost height of the vision of God through mental prayer. By renouncing the world for the sake of [salvation of] the world, by sacred silence of the mind, by mental quiet, by focusing the mind in unceasing divine prayer and attention, and by ascent through action to the vision of God She became for monks an example of a focused life for the benefit of the inward man. [Inward man in the sense of "yet the inward man is renewed day by day."(2 Cor.4:16)] Monks, who have renounced the world, can look at Her; imitate Her in this spiritual labour. Therefore they should make assiduous efforts as much as they can, but they can call upon Her for help, because She is a practitioner of mental prayer and She is instructed by the Holy Spirit. Who can now estimate the true worth of divine mental prayer if the Mother of God is, as aforementioned, Herself a practitioner of it?
There are those who have their doubts about it, as if it were something unverified and unreliable. It is time to remove these doubts and provide indubitable proof through the evidence of the God-bearing fathers, who wrote with the inspiration of God's grace, and the Holy Scriptures.
Saint Basil the Great, pillar of fire, mouth speaking with the fire of the Holy Spirit, explains the following verse from the divine Scripture: "I will bless the Lord at all times: his praise shall continually be in my mouth" (Ps. 33:1). He explains wonderfully what the mental mouth is and what mental actions are, with evidence from Holy Scripture. These are his very words which are full of Divine wisdom: "His praise

shall continually be in my mouth." It seems the prophet said something impossible: how can God's praise be in someone's mouth at all times? When a person speaks about simple everyday things, he does not have God's praise on his lips, and neither when sleeping, keeping silent, and also when eating and drinking, how could his mouth praise? In answer to that we say that the inner man has a certain mental mouth, with which he nourishes himself when he partakes of the Word of life, Which is the bread of God, which cometh down from heaven (Jn. 6:33). It is that very mouth about which the prophet said: "I opened my mouth and panted" (Ps. 118:131). This is what the Lord encourages us to do: to keep this mouth open to receive sufficient true food. He says: "Open thy mouth wide, and I will fill it" (Ps. 80:10). So once the thought of God is inscribed and consolidated in the mind of the soul, and is always there, it may be called praise of God. And according to the words of the apostle, a diligent person can do all to the glory of God, so that everything, every word and every mental action has the value of praise. "Whether therefore ye eat, or drink, or whatsoever ye do, do all to the glory of God" (1 Cor. 10:31). The heart of such a person is awake even when he is asleep." So speaks Saint Basil. From his words it is clear that in addition to the bodily mouth there is a mental mouth and mental action. Also there is mental praise which can be continuous, because it mentally takes place in the inner man. The great Macarius, universal sun, heavenly man, says about this holy prayer, "A Christian must always remember God, for it is written: "Thou shalt love the Lord thy God with all thy heart" (Mt. 22:37). Not only should he love the Lord when he enters a house of prayer, but also when travelling, talking, eating, and quenching his thirst. He should remember God and love him and aspire for Him, because He said, "For where your treasure is, there will your heart be also." (Mt. 6: 21)"

The venerable and God-bearing ancient holy Father Isaiah the Hermit says about innermost reflection, i.e., the Jesus prayer with one's thought in the heart, the following words from divine Scripture: "My heart was hot within me, while I was musing the fire burned." (Ps. 39:3)

Venerable Symeon shone with unspeakable gifts of the Holy Spirit and therefore the whole Church named him the New Theologian. In his sermon on the three forms of prayer he writes about mental prayer and attention : "Our holy fathers heard that the Lord said that out of the heart proceed evil thoughts, murders, adulteries, fornications, thefts, false witness, blasphemies and that these are the things which defile a man (Mt. 15:19-20), and again they heard that He instructs: "cleanse first that which is within the cup and platter, that the outside of them may be clean also." (Mt. 23:26) Then they dropped all other things and struggled only to guard the heart, knowing for certain that by this inner work they would more easily acquire also all the other virtues while without this inner work it is impossible to acquire and keep any virtue." These words of the saint clearly show that the divine fathers used those words of the Lord for themselves as evidence and foundation of the guarding of the heart, i.e., of mentally invoking Jesus. Venerable Simeon cites other verses from sacred Scriptures to testify about divine mental prayer: "Ecclesiastes talks about this also: "Rejoice, O young man, in thy youth; ...and walk in the ways of thine heart... Therefore remove sorrow from thy heart." (Eccl. 11:9-10), and: "Though a prince's anger should mount against thee, do not desert thy post" (Eccl. 10:4). That post he [King Solomon] calls the heart, as the Lord said: "It is from the heart that his wicked designs come" (Mt. 15:19). "... [N]either be ye of doubtful mind' (Lk. 12:29), i.e., do not waste your mind on useless worries. "Because strait is the gate, and narrow is the way, which leadeth unto life" (Mt. 7:14), also: "Blessed are the poor in spirit" (Mt.

5:3), i.e., those who do not harbour a single thought about this age. And the apostle Peter says, "Be sober, be vigilant; because your adversary the devil, as a roaring lion, walketh about, seeking whom he may devour(1 Pet. 5:8)." And the apostle Paul clearly writes to the Ephesians about protecting the heart, saying, "For we wrestle not against flesh and blood, but against principalities, against powers, against the rulers of the darkness of this world, against spiritual wickedness in high places" (Eph. 6:12)."

Our blessed and God-bearing Father Gregory of Sinai ascended through the inner work of this divine prayer to ultimate vision of God, and as a sun he shone with the gifts of the Holy Spirit on holy Mount Athos. He combined the teachings of the Spirit-bearing fathers and compiled a book full of special spiritual benefit. This book teaches to a greater degree of subtlety the divine prayer which is performed as a sacred rite by the mind in the heart, than all the other writings of the holy fathers. He cites in support of his words the following from sacred Scripture: "Thou shalt remember the Lord thy God" (Deut. 8:18), and also: "In the morning sow thy seed, and in the evening withhold not thine hand" (Eccl. 11:6 et al). "For if I pray in an unknown tongue (i.e. with my mouth), my spirit (i.e. my voice) prayeth, but my understanding is unfruitful... I will pray with the spirit, and I will pray with the understanding also... I had rather speak five words with my understanding"(1 Cor. 14:14-19). He also takes as a witness John of the Ladder by relating these words to the prayer: "The kingdom of heaven suffereth violence, and the violent take it by force" (Mt. 11:12), and also: "No man can say that Jesus is the Lord, but by the Holy Ghost" (1 Cor. 12:3 et al).

We have shown here by the grace of God that the God-bearing fathers, who were made wise by the instruction of the Holy Spirit, based their doctrine of mental prayer, which is secretly performed as a sacred rite by the mind in the inner man, on the firm foundation of the divine Scriptures of the New and old Testaments. They borrowed from there, as from an inexhaustible source, a lot of evidence.

Which orthodox Christian, when he sees this, could in the least doubt this Divine pursuance? Really, only those who obey the spirit of insensibility: who hear and see, but do not want to understand and know. But those who fear God and have any common sense, when they see the testimonies of so many witnesses, unanimously recognize that this Divine work has advantages over all other monastic feats. It is appropriate and seemly for the angelic monastic rank. To this inner work our divine fathers and many others have dedicated many respectful words full of spiritual wisdom. They teach inner psychological feat [warfare] against [man's] psychological [inner] enemies [passions, delusions, demons]. How to aim this spiritual sword and invincible flaming weapon: the name of Jesus, which guards the gates of the heart, at them, i.e., how to perform with the mind [mentally] the sacred rite of this divine Jesus prayer in the heart?

Finally, I must, though being the weakest with regard to my intelligence, with the help of God, write at least something from the teachings of the holy fathers about the fact that this sacred mental prayer is a spiritual art, and about what quality this sacred Jesus prayer has and what it does.

Let it be known that our divine fathers called this sacred mental, inner work of the praying mind an art. Saint John of the Ladder (Climacos) in Sermon 27 "On keeping silence", which teaches about the mystery of mental prayer, says: "If you did thoroughly study this art, then it is impossible for you not to know what I'm saying. Sitting in the high place, watch, if you are able to, and you will see then: how, when, and where from, and how many, and what villains come to you in order to enter [your inner: mind, heart] and to steal your fruits. This guard gets up to pray when he gets tired.

Then he sits down again and courageously takes up the inner work [of guarding] he was doing before."

Saint Hesychius, presbyter of Jerusalem says about this sacred prayer: "Sobriety[41] is a spiritual art that, with God's help, completely frees a person from passionate thoughts and words, and evil deeds" (Ch. 1).

Saint Nicephorus the Faster, teaching about mental prayer, says, "Come, and I will unveil to you the art, or better, the science, of an eternal, or better, a heavenly way of life, which leads a person easily and safely into a haven of dispassion."

We have shown that the holy fathers call this holy prayer an art. I think, because just as a person cannot learn an art by himself without a skilled master, it is impossible to learn this inner work of mental prayer without a skilled mentor. So the art is mastered, according to Saint Nicephorus, by many, if not all, through learning [from a mentor]. Rarely without instruction, but through suffering and the warmth of faith, they receive instruction from God.

Orthodox Christians, laymen and monks, need to daily carry out the church [prayer] rule according to the statutes and with the help of sacred church books. This prayer rule is like a contribution we must bring to the King of heaven. Anyone who is literate can read these aloud without any teaching. However to bring God the mysterious sacrifice of prayer with the mind in the heart is not possible without learning it first [from a mentor(s)] because it is a spiritual art as indicated above.

Being a spiritual art, it also constitutes the unceasing [inward] work of monks [and nuns], so that NOT ONLY because of their renunciation of the world and everything that is in the world; of their change of name at their tonsure; their different clothes, celibacy, purity, self-chosen poverty; secluded meals and habitation, BUT ALSO owing to the mental and spiritual attention towards the inward man and [mental] prayer monks [and nuns] possess an exclusive pursuance which distinguishes them from laymen.

Someone who wants to learn spiritual inward work must be prepared. He should live in blessed obedience, which is the solid and unshakable foundation of this divine prayer. Then he can be shown, using examples from the teaching of the holy fathers what the quality and effect of the sacred prayer are and what a great growth in all the virtues it causes in an ascetic. This strengthens his desire to work with great zeal at learning this sacred mental prayer

Saint John of the Ladder says in Sermon 28 "On prayer": "The quality of prayer is communication and unification with God, and its effect - a strengthened inner peace, reconciliation with God, mother and at the same time daughter of tears, the cleansing of sins, a bridge over temptations, a wall against sorrows, the end of [invisible] warfare[42], an angelic pursuance, the nourishment of all the bodiless spirits, future joy, the source of virtues, the cause of talents, invisible prosperity, food for the soul, illumination of the mind, poleaxe against despair, proof of hope, end of sorrow, riches of monks, treasure of those keeping silence, reduced irritability, the indication of a limit, the exposing of an inner state... For a person who truly prays prayer is trial, judgment and throne of the Lord, even before the [Last] Judgment[43] to come."

Saint Gregory of Sinai says in the 113th chapter: "Prayer in the beginner is like a fire of gladness that comes from the heart, in the perfect it is like the influence of fragrant light. Prayer is the preaching of the apostles, an act of faith, good tidings for those who hope, love realized, an angelic impulse, the power of the bodiless, a message to the heart, the hope of salvation, the sign of sanctification, the teaching of holiness, knowing God, engagement to the Holy Spirit, the rejoicing of Jesus, gladness of the soul, the mercy of God, the seal of Christ, a ray of the mental sun, the morning star of hearts, sign of reconciliation with God, the grace of God, the wisdom of God, the sign of an angelic way of life."

Saint Hesychius, presbyter of Jerusalem, said: "We can worthily and appropriately call the practice of guarding the mind light- and as lightning, refulgent and fiery. It surpasses, to tell the truth, all the countless bodily virtues. So this virtue should be called by the most worthy names because such effulgent light is born from it. When the sinful, indecent, vile, foolish, ignorant and unjust, come to love prayer of the heart, they can become righteous, pleasing, pure, saintly and sensible in Christ Jesus. And not only that, they can also see Divine mysteries and theologize. And, when they have become able to see, they move towards this pure and endless light and touch Him with unspeakable touch and live with Him and abide with Him. Since they tasted that "the Lord is good" (Ps. 33:8), such beginner-angels obviously fulfil the divine word of the prophet David: "Surely the righteous shall give thanks unto Thy name: the upright shall dwell in Thy presence(Ps. 140:13)."

Other God-bearing fathers speak of this sacred prayer in exactly the same way. In their teaching full of Divine wisdom they bear witness to its effect, to the unspeakable benefits that spring from it and to the acquisition of the Divine gifts of the Holy Spirit with its help.

If someone sees that this sacred prayer leads an ascetic to such heavenly riches of various virtues, he will burn with divine zeal to incessantly do the inner work of prayer, to always keep the Most Sweet Jesus in his mind and heart, to remember constantly His dearest name, and by this to burn with His unspeakable love. Except perhaps only someone who is a captive of worldly thoughts or who is bound by the concerns of the flesh, which leads many away and removes them from the Kingdom of God that is within us... But those who wish to be united by love to the Most Sweet Jesus will spit at all the

beauties of this world, all pleasures and bodily quiet. They will want to have nothing else in this life, but constantly be engaged in the heavenly inward work of this prayer.
Men and angels have the Jesus prayer in common. With this prayer people rapidly make their life alike to an angelic one. Prayer is the source of all good works and virtues and drives away the darkness of the human passions. If you acquire this prayer your soul will become angelic-like even before your death. Prayer is divine joy. This is the only truly precious sword, because there is no other such weapon with which you can cut demons so well. It scorches them as fire burns thorns. This prayer inflames the whole person like fire and brings him unspeakable joy and gladness, so that he from joy forgets about this life, and he considers all of this age rubbish and ashes.
Sobriety of mind that is illuminated thought is the result of dispassion, i.e., of purity, fasting, abstinence, the Jesus prayer, of not despairing, of moderate sleep and of the action of the Holy Spirit, when grace is given to us. With these virtues the mind purifies itself from darkness, rudeness, illusions and it becomes illuminated. Then the person becomes quick-witted, sensible and joyful. No one can stop the whirlpool of thoughts in any way, unless by the unceasing Jesus prayer, by remembering death and the future torments, by remembering and longing for the blessings to come, by attentive singing [of psalms and spiritual chants] or reading in private[the works of the holy fathers]...
Prayer and fasting repel all sinful thoughts, stop the flushing of the brain, keep the mind from mutiny, focus it and illuminate it. Prayer and fasting expel from a person unclean spirits and heal those who are raving, as the Lord said: "Howbeit this kind (demons) goeth not out but by prayer and fasting(Mt. 17:21)." Prayer and fasting clear a mind, which is often darkened by demons... Prayer with sobriety of mind and heart,

and guarding the mind puts an end to oblivion, like water extinguishes fire... Come to love prayer, sinners! If you are indecent and vile, you will become saintly and worthy. If you are foolish and careless, you will become wise and prudent. If you are unrighteous, you will become righteous. And what's more, you will also be contemplators, theologians and witnesses of the divine Mysteries. This will happen by the invocation of the name of the Lord Jesus Christ, the Son of God...
As a man can see his face in a mirror, so he can see with his mind the whole of his life in a sober and good prayer whether he lives a good or an evil life. Such a sober prayer drives away from a person the darkness of the passions. It frees a person of all demonic nets, thoughts, words and deeds. It conquers all desires stemming from one's lower nature. It conquers the senses and grief. And as regards all temptations, it helps to overcome them and to purify oneself of them and it slays them as a flaming sword, for God called with this name is the God to Whom all obey...
The beginning of this good and beautiful inward work consists in weakening the passions, not doing what is not pleasing to God, and not doing unto your brother what you yourself would hate them do unto you. Then guard your heart against carnal pleasure and vile burning passion. Firmly guard the mind against thoughts so that it always keeps the heart humble. From this a prayer is born that conquers and destroys a multitude of passions and evil spirits, and grace is augmented.
Fasting and the Jesus prayer purify and strengthen the [practice of] sobriety and attention. The other way around, also sobriety constitutes dignity, sanctity and a support for prayer. Sobriety can in another way be called purity of mind. Uncleanliness of mind is bad thoughts, and impurity of heart is burning passion and lascivious pleasure. The heart cannot stand fast in purity, and not defile itself, if it is not made con-

trite by fasting. Without fasting it is also impossible to keep saintliness, nor does the flesh subordinate itself to the spirit for spiritual activity, nor does even prayer itself rise up or have an effect, because natural needs prevail and the flesh is compelled to start burning with lust. When the flesh is burning with lust lascivious thoughts come that defile the mind. These thoughts in their turn excite the heart and it becomes defiled too. Because of this grace abandons us and the unclean spirits have the impertinence to rule over us as much as they want. They compel the flesh to passions and direct the mind to wherever they want, or, they keep it as if tied with a rope, incapable of spiritual desires and practices. Those evil spirits try at all costs to lead the mind into the dark and into oblivion, and then to plunge us into the abyss of sin. But we will always hold on to fasting, because it is a quiet refuge from the enemy's mental net. It purifies the body, nourishes and strengthens prayer, makes it strong, it [prayer] will come from the lips as a flame of fire. Sober prayer combined with fasting singes demons, so that they cannot come near a chaste soul to play mean tricks, just like you cannot come near a hot stove.

At a time when the enemy strongly disturbs you, when the soul is frightened, you should read psalms and prayers out loud, or combine prayer with handwork, so that your mind is on the work you are carrying out. Do not pay attention to what disturbs you in the least and do not fear, for God abides with us and the angel of the Lord never draws back from us... Demons especially oppose the Jesus prayer, because there is nothing that harms them and throws them in despondency like this prayer. The Jesus prayer is very scary for demons, for as fire scorches thorns, so does this prayer combined with fasting sear them and chase them away. Therefore they grow louder in order to take prayer away from you, but after they have bothered you a little they disappear like smoke in the

air and become invisible. If you prepare for prayer, prepare to battle with demons and arm yourself heavily to bravely withstand the attack that will come over you. Like wild beasts they will enter into battle against you and they will cause suffering to your whole body. They bring great trouble to those that keep vigil and diligently pray, because they see the weapon that can destroy their power. They cannot tolerate it, it makes them tremble and disappear, because of pain. We should throw off all negligence and cowardice and effeminacy. Like that we can resist demonic deceit. We should take pains to pray and to practice the other virtues. We should work with zeal and strength, soul, heart, mind. We should be similar to someone running on the road without looking back when a bystander says: "What a miser, he is keeping the fast!" For such is the cunning of demons. They are constantly studying us, and as a watchman they note down our inclinations and wishes: what we think and what we love, what we are doing. And to the passion they notice in us they will prompt us and such nets they will cast. In that way we ourselves arouse against ourselves all sorts of passion and we are its cause. So demons are looking for a pretext in us, through our own inclinations and desires we are more likely to get tangled up. What should be done so that the mind is always occupied with God? If you do not acquire these three virtues: love of God and people, abstinence and Jesus prayer, then our mind cannot be fully occupied with God; for love tames anger, lust is weakened by abstinence, and prayer distracts the mind from thoughts and banishes all hatred and haughtiness. Indeed, be constantly occupied by God, for God will teach you everything and He will reveal by the Holy Spirit the highest, the heavenly, and the lowest, the earthly.
May the Lord God help us and may He save us by His grace in the ages. Amen.

Endnotes

Life

1 The vocation of archpriest (protopresbyter) in the capacity of rector went out of use in the beginning of the XIXth century. Protopresbyters in counties and provinces always occupied the office of chairman of Spiritual councils, of rectors, etc. They enjoyed the special confidence of the eparchial authorities.

2 Sylvester Kulyabko (secular name Simeon, born in 1701 or 1704, died in 1761). He passed the full course of the Kiev academy, became a monk, taught rhetoric, philosophy and theology at the academy. In 1744, as rector of the academy, archimandrite Sylvester was sent to Saint- Petersburg to congratulate the newly-wed grand- duke Peter Fyodorovich and grand- duchess Catherine Alekseyevna. Empress Elizabeth liked the two sermons he delivered: he was retained in Saint- Petersburg, and then elevated to the rank of bishop of Kostroma, and in 1750 to the rank of archbishop of Saint- Petersburg.

3 Cellarer (translated from the Greek word for "pantry"). Head of the monastery table, the pantry with victuals.

4 Penance (translated from the Greek word for "punishment") - spiritual punishment, correction.

5 Hieromonk: priest-monk.

6 Timothy (in the world Tikhon Ivanovich Shcherbak or Shcherbatsky, 1698-1767). At the end of the course at the academy he became a monk and in 1737 he received the position of cathedral clerk at the Sophia monastery in Kiev. In the same year he was promoted to hegoumen and appointed father superior of the Mharsky Transfiguration of the Saviour monastery of the Poltava eparchy. Here he stayed for a short time, for the same year he moved back to Kiev to the Vydubychi monastery. In 1739, he was ordained archimandrite and appointed hegoumen of the Saint Michael's Golden-Domed monastery, and April 14, 1740 he was confirmed to be the father superior of the Kiev Lavra of the Caves. As directed by the Empress Elizabeth Petrovna, November 9, 1747 he was appointed metropolitan of Kiev. On November 4, 1754 he became member of the synod. As of 1764 he was the metropolitan of Moscow and Kaluga.

7 The economo is the brother at the head of the monastery housekeeping. He directs the work of all who are engaged in a household obedience.

8 Hieroschemamonk: a schemamonk who has been ordained a priest.

9 Bondservant

10 Moldawallachia - Moldavia and Wallachia, Danubian principalities. In the XVI century, they became vassal states of the Ottoman Empire, but they retained their statehood. Nowadays Moldova and Romania.

11 Archimandrite Basil (Gondikakis). Father superior of the Iviron monastery on mount Athos (1990-2005), author of

several books and articles of spiritual content. He currently lives in retirement.

12 Venerable Basil Polyanomerulsky (±1692-1767) was a highly revered elder in the Moldawallachia lands and on Mount Athos. He was canonized by the holy synod of the Romanian church October 5, 2003. His name was entered in the menologion of the Russian Orthodox Church by decision of the holy synod of the ROC on August 21, 2007.

13 Stavrophore. This degree is also known as the Little Schema.

14 Paraklesis (Greek: "consolation") is a moleben canon, dedicated to the Virgin, which is sung and read when the soul is grieving.

15 The meek Païssy at that time thought only of obedience and monasticism, but not of priesthood.

16 Athos was then still under Turkish rule. They demanded of the monasteries payment of taxes, which brought them to complete ruin. The monks left their monasteries because of it.

17 Lev. Currency unit.

18 Letters patent (no singular form exists) are a type of legal instrument in the form of a published written order issued by a monarch or president, generally granting an office, right, monopoly, title, or status to a person or organization.

19 Guest house.

20 Here: canon - a rule of prayer.

21 Panagia. Pan hagios. All-holy. A title of the Mother of God.

22 Grief and suffering.

23 The non-possessors (нестяжатели, nestiazhateli), led by venerable Nilus of Sora (1433-1508), demanded the church to reject "hoarding" (i.e., acquisition of land and property) as contrary to the Gospel. The possessors (стяжатели, stiazhateli), headed by Joseph Volotsky (±1439-1515) defended the principle of the inviolability of church and monastery lands. Despite the moral attraction of non-possessing it should be recognized that, taken to the extreme, it could endanger the normal flow of church and monastic life.

24 Advent.

25 In the sense of taking care of the salvation of our souls.

26 Hesychasm: the practice of inner prayer, prayer in the mind while the mind it is focused in the heart. It originates from the prayer of the Mother of God. Practiced by the Egyptian desert fathers, it was revived by Saint Gregory Palamas.

27 Exegesis - explanation, interpretation in order to identify as precisely as possible the meaning of the text.

28 Hierarch Ignatius Bryanchaninov, Caucasian bishop (1807-1867). He came from a noble family and received an excellent secular education. He became a novice in the Alexander-Svirsky monastery. He then moved with his elder, hieromonk Leonid (Leo) to the Optina monastery. From him he took his love for patristic literature. At that time in Optina

they had collected numerous handwritten translations of venerable Païssy, and the Philokalia (Dobrotolyubie) had already been published. In his writings and letters hierarch Ignatius revealed all the subtleties of the spiritual life. He is often called the founder of modern Russian spiritual literature.
29 Bishop Arsenius (Stadnitskii) (1862-1936) was born in Moldavia. He graduated from the Kiev theological academy. From 1898 he was the rector of the Moscow theological academy. He was ordained bishop of Volokolamsk and appointed vicar of the Moscow metropolitanate in 1899. From 1903 he was bishop of Pskov. He studied the history of the Moldavian church. He defended his dissertation for a doctorate in theology in 1904. From 1907 he was archbishop. In the history of the Russian church the name of archbishop Arsenii stands next to the name of patriarch Tikhon. Together with him and metropolitan Anthony (Khrapovitsky) he was a candidate for the patriarchal throne. November 29, 1917 he was elevated to the rank of metropolitan. In 1927, he became a permanent member of the temporary patriarchal synod. In 1933 he was appointed metropolitan of Tashkent.

30 The Tismana monastery, one of the oldest in Wallachia, was located in mountainous surroundings and founded in the 70's of the XIVth century by venerable Nicodemus, the Pious of Tismana (±1310-1406, from Great Wallachia, Macedonia).

31 Gregory Tsamblak (±1364-±1450), metropolitan of Kiev and then of Moldawallachia. Educated in Constantinople. His writings have enjoyed great prestige among the Russian, Bulgarian and Serbian clergy.

32 Hierarch Demetrius, metropolitan of Rostov (1651-1709). He compiled the famous menaion (lives of the saints, compiled by date according to the menologium), which in the

XVIIIth century became the favourite books of pious Christians.
33 Alexander the Good. Ruler of Moldavia from 1400 to 1432.

34 Praise to the most holy God-Mother (Saturday of the Akathist) takes place in the 4th Week of Lent.

35 Ethnic group of Western Ukrainians.

Doctrine

36 According to your own understanding.

37 Knowingly violating the blessing given by the confessor.

38 "Now it came to pass, as they went, that he entered into a certain village: and a certain woman named Martha received him into her house. And she had a sister called Mary, which also sat at Jesus' feet, and heard his word. But Martha was cumbered about much serving, and came to him, and said, Lord, dost Thou not care that my sister hath left me to serve alone? Bid her therefore that she helps me. And Jesus answered and said unto her, Martha, Martha, thou art careful and troubled about many things: But one thing is needful: and Mary hath chosen that good part, which shall not be taken away from her" (Lk. 10:38-42).

39 The ranks of the angels, the celestial, bodiless powers.

40 Silence is a state of mind not troubled by thoughts, the silence of freedom from passions, light contemplation, partaking of the mysteries of God (Venerable John of the Ladder).

41 Sobriety is a Christian virtue which consists in a careful attitude to spiritual life, i.e., in keeping oneself from sin by incessant appeal to God. Sobriety is a manifestation of unceasing spiritual vigilance on the path of salvation.

42 Invisible, spiritual battle is the struggle against the passions and overcoming temptations.

43 The Last Judgment at the time of the Second Coming of the Lord Jesus Christ.

Lightning Source UK Ltd.
Milton Keynes UK
UKHW011839020820
367582UK00001B/10

9 789079 889136